Reserved For Emperors

Reserved For Emperors

Selected Blogs

January 2005 Through June 2006

Aaron Dietz

ISBN 978-1-84728-801-1

Book Design :: Aaron Dietz
Cover :: Erik Tosten

Thanks to all of my readers.

Thanks to the following for their various forms of support:

Tara Bannon, Kate, BiBi Cambridge, Jeremy Chapman, Mr. Chung,
Shaina Cohen, Q.C., Corrine Davis, Bill Dawes, Suzy (my first subscriber),
my parents and sisters, Frank Greer, H, Brian Howard, Bree, Joaquin Liebert,
Scotty McMullan, Moira, Collin Moon, Tim and Karrie, Dave Prosper, Kirby,
Kevin Palmer, Randy Palmer, TR, Jamal River, Sarah: A Fugitive Warlord,
Angela Sigg, Slacksploitation, Gary Robert Smith II, James Smith, Stupidhead,
Bryan Tomasovich, Erik Tosten, Sweet Tourné, David and Sophea,
James P. Wainscotting, Todd Williamson, and everyone in the writer's groups.

If you want to save time,
skip to page 227.

Otherwise,

proceed

in

random

fashion.

The New Chronology

blog
Paris
corporation
commission
Lagavulin
poo
penis
cooking
once
walk
sheep
time
games
dialogs
disaster
white tea
gum
panties
aliens
dream
driving
sports
earthquake
hero
shoelace
language
BEEP
THE

The Beginning

In the beginning, I hated blogs. They were trite, predictable, poorly written, poorly spelled, and about a thousand other things that were just wrong. But I was poking around on the Internet one day when I discovered a blogger who went by the name of Humble B. Wonderful. My world view shifted.

Here was someone using the blog as a format (rather than a style of writing), fearlessly reinventing and expanding the blog genre while rescuing it from stylistic and contextual dogma.

Humble B. Wonderful's writing was original and fresh. Irreverent and smart. And hilarious. I could never have conceived of writing blogs of my own without knowing that such genius was possible. I left the raw originality of the early Humble B. Wonderful posts unchallenged, but a modest success at blogging helped me decide to turn writing into a career. I have Humble B. Wonderful to thank for that.

I've edited these blogs. I have no intention of preserving the original post in this book, since I consider all of my writing unfinished and therefore subject to improvement. In many cases, what you see on the page is exactly what is available online. The rest of the time, they are usually close enough that you probably won't notice the difference.

You will notice that to the left of most of the blogs in this book, there is a small amount of expository material. This is like an audio commentary that you would find on a DVD, except that you have to read it. It will sometimes not make sense to read it first, much as listening to the audio commentary on a movie might not be the first way you want to watch it. If you're the type that likes audio commentaries, read each blog, then read the related commentary. If you don't like them, skip the commentaries. If you've read and memorized every blog I've ever written, only read the commentaries. Or do whatever you want, because that's what you'll do, right?

Perhaps it *would* be harder to become the premier composer in this world than it would be to get an acceptance letter from a decent independent book publisher, but there is a definite *perceived* statistical similarity between these two potential events. In any case, now this book is out, so I guess becoming a composer wasn't necessary after all!

I wrote this while I was reading a book about a group of composers and was surprised to find that so many of them were anti-Semitic—to the point that they actually wrote books about how Jewish people were destroying music. It's always frustrating to learn about these things, but never really that surprising.

I will move to Paris and learn the piano

It is my new plan.

After becoming a 31-year-old virtuoso, I will become a brilliant composer, because I've learned that back in the day, many composers were allowed to publish books. And I want to publish mine. Collecting rejection letters is a good pastime, but I think I'm ready to give that up in order to become a published author.

Yes, great composers such as Liszt and Mendelssohn, for example, put out books on all sorts of subjects. They wrote books on music, books on Jews, books on how Jews were ruining music....

I will have many obstacles in my way, such as:

1. Becoming the world's foremost piano player and composer.
2. Overcoming the biases of a world that has moved on to other styles of music.
3. Overcoming the world's apparent inability to buy books by composers that have nothing to do with anti-Semitism.

However, I figure this is still easier than finding a publisher the normal way.

I didn't move to Paris, but I did move to Seattle.

Having given notice at my job in Denver, I felt comfortable posting this blog, which is a copy of an email I wrote to a friend.

Like a lot of my writing, there is truth in it, but it's not meant to be entirely accurate. While there was a lot of mystery as to what my actual job was, I did work hard.

Fire Me Please

A friend emailed me while I was at work. "What do you actually do?" he asked.

Here is my response:

I spend a good deal of time trying to recover my self-esteem.

Other parts of my day are spent on making tea, visiting with fellow employees, going out to eat, keeping up to date with what's on our Web site, checking IMDb for upcoming DVD releases (MacGyver, Season 1, baby!), pre-ordering stupid shit I don't need from Amazon, rearranging my Netflix queue, answering my own personal phone line, as well as a great deal of other various important tasks.

For example, at the end of every pay period, I scribble in enough hours to total 40 a week on my time sheet. At the end of each month, I have to advance my calendar forward a page. Occasionally, I have to check my voice mail when the little red light is on. Also, I must never forget to make sure I have requested the correct time off whenever I'm planning a trip—sometimes this means I must check the large work calendar several times a day for a week or more (one can never be too sure).

I try to pay close attention to how my desk looks, too. Have the same papers been on top of the pile the whole week? Have I been rotating in enough technical-reading-type books? Have I left them open on different pages than last week? It's important to have a well-circulated desk arrangement.

Then, of course, there are breaks and snack times, but I am not one to cheat my fellow taxpayers. If I have to stay late to get my twenty minutes worth of work done for that day, then that's what I am prepared to do once in a while (like when I'm waiting for a ride that has warned me they will be late).

Diligence, perseverance and success, with no less dignity than the City Librarian. That's my motto!

This is actually pretty true. It happened years ago while I lived in Denver. The test wasn't "mandatory" per se, but I don't think anyone refused to take it.

The fact of the matter is, I was simply following directions. The directions said to leave the answer blank if there wasn't a choice that I could comfortably agree with, so I left about two thirds of the test blank.

I was impressed when they handed me my actual score sheet back, so I could just fill in the ones that I didn't fill in before. The second time I left nothing to chance: I answered every question even if it was against what the directions told me to do. I was going to leave evidence of a personality even if I had to lie and cheat to do it!

I took a personality test and failed

It's true.

I took the Myers-Briggs personality test at the "request" of my former employer. I received the results back saying they could not detect a personality.

Honest.

My employer made me re-take the test until some semblance of a personality emerged.

I moved to Seattle and had trouble finding a good job (or even a bad one), so I thought this was a good way to kill two birds with one stone. Not that I'd actually ever stone a bird, but you know what I mean.

This may not sweeten the deal at all but I will totally put out in addition to doing data entry

So...give me a job.

I did get a job, finally. It was a dreadful position, one that I eventually quit. It wasn't really that bad, relatively—I've worked much worse. But I was also sort of examining myself and what I wanted to do with my life and working temp jobs for corporations just didn't sound good. Eventually, I decided I'd rather be out on the street than spend time in that building.

The job did give me some great fodder to write about, though. This next blog in particular was about a phenomenon that baffled me completely. I saw so many overweight people in that building flocking to the free junk food as soon as it was placed on the table. Similarly, the stairs were open for use, yet many people still used the elevator to go up one story. To live in such a contradictory mind set is the definition of working at a corporation.

On the subject of weight: I'm skinny. I just can't keep it on me. It's been a struggle.

Yay! The Corporation makes me fatter!

My life-long struggle to gain weight could well be over, for I have come across a remarkable solution: work for The Corporation!

Move those fingers! Shuffle those papers! That is all the exercise you will get, when you work for The Corporation!

Ooh! Lookie! Free high-carb snacks, sugary sweets and carbonated sugar drinks wheeled in daily to keep us typing fast! It's GOOD to work for The Corporation!

No fruit for you!

Now I have eleven adequate years to enjoy before my fatal heart attack!

I spent about a month at The Corporation, but already, at day eleven, I was becoming one of the brainwashed minions. I did escape frequently to the nearest park to read a book and eat lunch, but my lunch period grew longer each day as I cared less and less about working there. One day the lunch period didn't end.

Will I listen to myself?!

Eleven days working as a temp in Corp-O-Landia and already I'm brainwashed.

Here I am, turning in my security badge at the end of the day:

The security guard says, "How's it going?"

I answer, "A lot better *now*."

In my currently brainwashed state, I think this is funny. But in reality, we've had this conversation before and probably will again. We are corporate slaves: unoriginal and thoughtless.

However, deep down, I like to think that we are speaking in code. It is as if we are saying to each other, "Yep, all my dreams and aspirations have been crushed. How about you?"

There's a line in *Basic Instinct* where a
supporting character says something like,
"That magna cum laude pussy done fried
up your brain, hoss!" That's what I'm
referring to in this blog.

I am just like that guy in *Basic Instinct*

Except it weren't no pootang that done fried my brain, it were the radiation comin' offa' mah monitor-thingy at my fancy corporate job, hoss!

This is absolutely true. There really was a "missing" floor and before I left the job, I asked about it. I won't tell you what it really was. Sometimes the truth is less important than what our imaginations create.

It's also true that I heard a security guard holler, "I'm on my way," only to find him in the break room minutes later, eating a snack by himself.

The Mysteries of...The Corporation!!!

What is between the fourth and fifth floors? To go from the fifth floor to the sixth, I go up two flights of stairs. Back and forth.

But to go from the fifth floor to the fourth, I go back and forth—and back and forth again. Four flights of stairs! And it is not a floor with super high ceilings so I know there's something missing!

Nobody asks because they are drones and they use the elevator anyway. I bet the security guards know, though!

I saw one talk into his radio on my way to the cafeteria for break. He said, "I'm on my way."

It sounded important. I wondered where he was headed that could be so important!

Behold and lo! He was in the break room when I got there! He took a sneaky way because he can. He's a security guard!

I think maybe he's spying on me. They are suspicious of people that are suspicious of them. And I take the stairs, which makes me seem *double* suspect.

I hope they don't have secret prison cells on the mystery floor because I think they will try to put me in one!

This is that rare sort of delight—the kind that makes you laugh even though you are in "Hell." I was sorting faxes and clearly someone had meant to start their greeting off with, "Hello," yet what they put was perhaps more honest.

I promptly circled it so that anyone handling that fax would know where they were working. I wish I had photocopied it.

I discover the true nature of...The Corporation!!!

I received and sorted a fax today that let slip a ghastly secret—one that The Corporation surely doesn't want us to know!

On the fax, clear as day, was the secret behind this terrible place. All at once, I knew why working there churned my stomach so. Yes, all things were explained to me.

The fax began with these simple words:

> *Hell, can you please fax me...*

It was so obvious yet I missed it! I work in Hell!

And what do they do in Hell? They process insurance claims and refinance mortgages! And probably a few things have just been explained to you as well.

It's true that I walked around with my fly open
quite often at The Corporation. I'm just not used
to having so many snaps and hooks and whatnot
to worry about.

However, I have gained some weight
(though not from working at The Corporation—
from eating right and weight training) and I no
longer have as much of a pants buying problem.

Just to set the record straight—I actually
like to dress up, but I feel like if you're going to do
it, you should go all out. I'd rather wear a three-
piece suit than just a shirt and tie. This might
be partly because of the killer three-piece suit I
picked up at a vintage store in Denver. I bought
it and had it slightly tailored for under $90. It's
beautiful.

Hey Kids, Dressing Up Everyday Sucks!

It's not that I'm opposed to visiting the dry cleaners or meeting Asian neighbors. In fact, I may never have met Mr. Chung, who is actually from Hawaii, if I hadn't gotten a job at The Corporation. I'm happy to give him business.

However, I am skinny. And they don't make pants for my length and my slim waistline outside of Iowa. I guess that's where all the long-legged, slim boys grow. So, because I can't afford to fly to Des Moines to do my shopping, all my pants are short by two inches and this makes me self-conscious.

Also, because of my long-leggedness, if I tuck my shirt in, I look like my chest is about a foot high. Truly, this freaks people out. So I prefer not to wear the dress clothes because tucking in is mandatory at The Corporation.

One last thing: those pants are so complicated! Some have an extra hook, or a snap and a hook and then there's a belt involved because I do like to wear the complete outfit, you know. So because of all this complication, I often forget to zip up and I walk around the office with my fly gaping open.

Jeremy was stationed in Iraq at the time, which left him so few options for entertainment that he was forced to read my blogs. I posted about how I quit my job and was going to be a writer or go homeless trying. He read the post and wrote me, saying, "You must need money. If I give you a dollar, will you write about how great I am?"

It sounded like a fun assignment, so I said yes. I wrote the piece and he mailed the dollar to me (tipping me 250 Iraqi dinars!).

His one dollar request gave me the idea to offer myself as a cheap freelancer, though I decided to double the price after each commission. I continue to accept commissions based on this pricing system (details are available at aarondietz. us) and since then I've been commissioned for many interesting projects, from writing someone's obituary to coming up with the answer to the question, "Where do I see myself in ten years?" (for someone else, mind you—not where I, personally, see myself in ten years).

Jeremy asked that I target this piece toward a non-specific female audience, so it is sort of a persuasive paper.

Oh yes, almost forgot—during a trip to L.A. this past year, I got to meet Jeremy in person and he is, just as my essay suggests, great.

Jeremy Is Great

Jeremy[1] is, of course, great, just in case you didn't read the title. What is the number one reason he's great? He's "a damn funny guy with superb writing skills." Those are his own words, so you *know* it's true!

Also, he's a Marine. How much more badass can you get? What, you want a SEAL? Forget it. Didn't you watch *The Abyss*? They freak out too much and every time they freak out they find a nuke and want to use it. Nothing wrong with Marines, though. Yeah, a Marine is what you want.

Yep, and he's a pilot, which means he's not just a huge mass of muscle-flesh. He has to know how to punch buttons and stuff. Plus, he's decorated with Air Medals and a Purple Heart. What are Purple Hearts given out for? He had to get hurt to get it—wounded somehow. Either that or he had to have done some pretty awesome, badass, meritorious thing. Or both. How much more of a tough guy do you want?!

No, but I know—you want a nice guy, too. Not just some muscle bound hunk of manhood. He's got to be a nice person. Not gay or anything, but a nice guy. That's Jeremy. He's definitely not gay, but he won't beat up your gay friends (at least not for them *being* gay). I mean it (see source[2])!

More evidence that Jeremy's a nice guy? Simple: he puts the toilet seat down. Honest (see source[3]).

I'd probably hate him for being one of those manly men I don't get along with except that he's also mega fucking smart. And smart people are entertaining. Oh, I'm sure he's buff and all, but let's face it—throw a guy in a tux for a formal night out and they all look the same. On those rare occasions, you want the man to say something interesting, am I right? That's Jeremy! He can tell you how to see the future in a slushee (see source[4]) or regale you with humorous tales of drunken abandon (see source[5]).

Yeah, occasionally I get messages from people that read my blogs, people writing in saying, "Hi," or, "You're funny." Well, Jeremy's messages are all intelligent and shit and he's all checking out my Web site and pointing out shit on a story that I didn't really notice before. He once said that he was a "delightful respite to beleaguered blogging icons." And that would be a very conceited thing for him to say except that he's absolutely right. He's funny and more interesting than a lot of people that send me messages (not that it's a contest, but it's true).

Yep. But really, he's a nice guy, he is. He likes helping people. I'm not asking you to take my word for it, though: he once helped a girl get her air conditioner working again (she was about to die of heat exhaustion). And it wasn't because he was trying to get into her pants, either, because she's a lesbian (see source[6]). See? Really, he is a nice guy.

Did I mention he's a nice guy?

And his hair—is not going to be talked about in this essay. But you can see that he's not ugly by looking at his photos (see photos[7]), which also serve as proof that he's capable of holding small children without injuring them.

To sum up: Marine, funny, writer, nice guy, not gay. Jeremy is great.

1 Jeremy's blogs can be found at: www.myspace.com/captainavenger

2 This was a link to a blog of Jeremy's that was written in support of gay rights. It contained hilarious observations like, "the more gay men out there, the more chicks for me."

3 This was a reference to a blog by Jeremy, in which he explains that he puts the seat *and lid* down in order to enact a sneaky revenge on women that require men to put the seat down.

4 This link went to a blog of his that explained just that: how to see the future in a slushee.

5 I won't embarrass Jeremy by telling you what this link was all about.

6 This link went to a blog written by Slacksploitation, who is indeed a lesbian. She was having a problem with her air conditioner and Jeremy talked her through troubleshooting the problem and fixing it, all from his post in Iraq. What a handy Marine!

7 This link went to a series of photos, one of which showed Jeremy holding his daughter.

This was the $8 commission in my price-doubling freelance system. A reader that went by the name of Sarah: A Fugitive Warlord wanted me to "make some shit up," which left things fairly ambiguous. The job turned out to be pretty easy, since I came up with so many great gags just by using her online name. It's a sweet, funny piece and it's one of my favorites.

Sarah: A Fugitive Warlord claims that she is nothing like the character in this story, which made it even funnier to her.

An Evening With Sarah: A Fugitive Warlord

Sarah shows up as I'm making dinner. She's a fugitive warlord, as you know, and here's the thing about fugitive warlords: they are always looking for a place to crash. I mean, they're on the run, you know? Fugitives!

So, I'm like, "Okay, yeah, I don't mind if you stay here—but just one night, okay? And that's it."

"Don't tell ME how many nights I'll be staying!" she says.

Here's the thing about warlords in general: they're bossy. Oh my, yes. They are definitely used to getting their way. They are warlords, after all.

I know better than to argue with a warlord, so I go back to making dinner. I have garlic and asparagus sizzling in a frying pan and I'm about to add some chopped olives when she says, "You are NOT putting olives in that!"

I say, "Look, Sarah, you may be a warlord and everything, but in MY kitchen, I'M the boss."

I add the olives.

"That's one night in the brig for refusing to follow orders!" she shouts. I roll my eyes, but I look away first so she can't see me do it.

We have a decent dinner. Fortunately, I always make a ton of pasta so there is plenty to go around. Her manners aren't bad, but when she wants something, it's "More parmesan!" or "More pepper!" Warlords don't say please or thank you.

After dinner, I try to interest her in a DVD or some music as entertainment, but no, she just wants to talk military strategy (BORING!).

After an hour or two I somehow get her talking about her private life and she suddenly whips out several snapshots—her favorite battle ax, an aerial photo of her all-time most defendable square mile of land, that sort of thing.

Suddenly, she stands up and proclaims, "It is time for the nightly Scotch!"

Now, fortunately I do have Scotch. I didn't know warlords required a nightly Scotch, but I'm pleased that I just so happen to be able to accommodate her.

I bring out a nice 16 year Lagavulin. It runs between $63 and $85 a bottle, depending on one's geographic location and the whims of the maker. I pour a healthy sized shot for each of us and after taking a good whiff of the wonderfully unique, smoky aroma, I set them on the coffee table.

Sarah instantly downs hers in one gulp.

"Sarah, that's good Scotch! You're supposed to sip it!"

She doesn't listen to me. Instead, she grabs the second shot and sucks that down, too.

"That one was for me!"

"Silence!" she shouts. "I demand silence for ten seconds!"

She coughs a little bit. I stand there, silently, for ten seconds, because you really can't argue with a warlord.

"I demand another nightly Scotch!" she says.

"Look, if you have three every night, you can't call each one a nightly Scotch."

She stares at me, trying to determine if I'm being insolent or just advising her.

"Um," I say, "why don't we just switch to beer? I have a couple PBR's."

I fish around in the fridge and pull them out.

Sarah stands up, already swaying a little bit. I hand her a can.

"I command you to open it," she says, handing it back.

"Okay, whatever you say."

I pop it open and she grabs it, guzzling it hastily. Most of it winds up on her shirt and on my hardwood floor.

"Watch it! You're making a mess!" I set my beer down and go to the kitchen for a rag, but while I'm in there I can hear her opening my can and dribbling that all over the floor, too.

I start wiping it up while she stands, unconcerned, in the middle of the mess.

"Now," she says, "I require dessert!"

I wince. I was afraid of that. I have absolutely nothing for dessert in the whole apartment. I just wasn't expecting a warlord this evening.

So, I stand up, beer still coating the floor, and I say, "There is nothing for dessert."

"No dessert? You cur! There will be an extra shtrong punishment for having no deshert!"

"Uh...okay."

"I shentence you to fight shomeone...to the death!"

She looks around the room. I live alone, so there really aren't many options.

"You," she says, pointing at me, "fight yourshelf...to the death!"

"Sarah, I'm not fighting myself to the death."

"If you will not fight to the death, then...."

She thinks for a few seconds while I go back to wiping up the beer.

"Men!" she announces. "Take him to the guillotine!" She's pointing at me, of course.

Naturally, there are no men to take me to the guillotine so I sit back from my cleanup to watch this realization spread across her face.

"Very well," she says, recovering gracefully. "I will reshign to my quartersh for the evening to decide how to deal with the likesh of you."

I just sit there, holding the beer soaked rag, waiting to see what she'll do next.

"You sir! Where are my quartersh?" she asks. There is more pointing involved.

I just nod my head toward the loveseat.

"Very well. Fold it out immediately!"

"It...doesn't fold out. That's it."

She stumbles over to the loveseat and stares at it.

Swaying back and forth, she says, "Of coursh. I am dishpleased with your level of commitment to our army. If I decide to let you live tomorrow morning, consider yourshelf demoted five timesh."

"Okay."

And with that, she collapses in the loveseat. I finish the beer cleanup and toss the rag in the kitchen sink.

"If you need anything, I'll just be...uh...in the brig, there," I say, pointing to my bedroom.

But Sarah, the fugitive warlord, is already snoring. Her eyes are eerily half-open and drool is pooling up in one corner of her mouth. I throw a blanket over her and head for bed.

Houston,
I will make everything I say more dramatic!

I will do this by saying, "Houston" before everything I say. Hey, it works for the astronauts!

> "Houston, I have a problem."
> "Houston, I'll have an iced latte and the key to the bathroom."
> "Houston, I'm going to be late for work today."
> "Houston, it is pronounced 'How-ston' in New York City."
> "Houston, I seem to be venting something out of my butt."

Now you try!

Scotch tastes bad. Anyone that doesn't agree has simply forgotten.

Here's how that happens. You drink Scotch. You get drunk. You have good times. You start to associate the taste of Scotch with good times.

In the case of Lagavulin, the kind of drunk that one such as me gets is much more spectacular than it is with any other kind of alcoholic beverage. For me, it really does make old jazz songs sound new again.

But don't drink. It's bad for you.

I am the heart and soul of Lagavulin

I am

I smell like smoke

I taste like ass

And I act like I'm 16 years old

Most of the time I inspire belligerence...or laziness

But on the most beauteous of nights I can make crickets sing in harmony

I can make old jazz records sound brand new

And I can make you love the pulse of life once again

This is based on a real experience, though I didn't
wait until I was home to write it. I started writing
while I watched the show, knowing already what
I wanted to put down. So it didn't exactly happen
as it says. I wasn't even all that drunk.

Do not drink and blog

It can only lead to embarrassment.

I know—it always sounds like a good idea at the time. But don't.

The next morning you'll read some blog you wrote about the Brazilian singer you saw the previous night. You'll mention her gorgeous voice of course, but mostly you'll focus on her small, waif of a body and her tiny, perky tits underneath her t-shirt, her sexy, hair-swaying shoulder and hip movements. You'll not forget to mention, of course, her adorable accent.

But that's the least of the embarrassing things you'll have drunkenly written for all to read.

You'll have a lengthy description of your fantasized future life with the poor Brazilian musician. You'll have it all laid out—how you sweep her off her feet with your clumsiness and how she doesn't drink and requires all her boyfriends to give up drinking so you do, immediately, but then months later you have a very bad day and she says in her Brazilian accent, "Let's go out and get you drunk, huh? Just dis once?" and you head out and get drunk and have the time of your life because she is so wonderful and makes you so happy and then one year later, when the relationship is starting to sour, you get in a fight and you stop the fight to ask if you can just go out and get drunk like that one night when you were so happy and she will shake her head and say, "No," because by then it will be over and she will know it but *you will not* so your heart will break into tiny pieces and get sprinkled across the continent like little Johnny Appleseeds only they will never grow into anything.

So do not drink and blog.

Trust me. I have told you exactly what will happen.

I get really annoyed at having to pee all the time.
And even eating gets bothersome. I'm always
having to stop work to make some food. I could
be way more productive if I didn't have to do these
menial tasks. Truly, life is challenging, but most
of it...is more along the lines of tedius.

This is one of those blogs that I was afraid
people would take too seriously. I thought maybe
they'd think I was really depressed, because to me
it's sort of a depressing little poem. But no, people
thought it was hilarious.

Everything is such a chore

Eating, drinking, sleeping, waking

Cooking, cleaning

Pooping, peeing

Putting stamps on letters

Removing the safety seal

Etc.

At some point in the middle of 2005, I started to
get a fair number of readers. My sister and I were
talking about it, discussing how people would
react positively to whatever I put up, no matter
what it was. She said something like, "You could
just put up a piece of crap and they'd love it."

I sort of took the challenge literally, and it
was well received. At the time, it was perhaps my
most popular blog ever. Though, in defense of my
fans and their taste in blogs—I actually like this
one quite a bit. I had meant it to be a little more...
crappy. But it turned out to be pretty funny, or at
least to me it was. In any case, I learned that poop
humor is still popular, something that Mel Brooks
has been saying (in different words, however)
virtually all his life.

Okay, I will take a dump now

And you are all invited!

Schwoop! There go my pants. Yes, my boxers are a paisley print today, but most of them are actually plaid.

Now I will pee a little.

Okay, all done. Now, to squeeze one out!

Here it comes.... Okay, everything's going well so far....

Nope, it's stuck. Crap! I hate it when that happens. Oh, I don't want to have to pinch it off! Please just keep going, little turd!

Ah, okay. It's being cooperative now. What a nice little poo!

Whew! Glad that's over. Okay, you can all go now. Hey, did you hear me? Leave. No, I will not let you look at it—that's gross!

Bill Dawes remains the only comedian who has
ever bought a joke from me. I got to meet him in
L.A. and confirm what I was beginning to suspect
from knowing him online and talking to him on
the phone: that he is a nice guy.

I caught his show and he's quite funny.
The fact that he allowed me to publish this blog
online, and again in a book, shows that he is also a
good sport. I'm sure if he had written it, it'd be a
lot funnier.

In this blog, I particularly like the line, "I
only gave you my number because I thought you
were sane."

My Best Friend, Bill Dawes!

Recently my best friend, Bill Dawes, gave me his cell phone number! I was so excited because we've never met in real life or anything, so now I could finally hear his voice and interact with him outside of the Internet! Recently, I've been institutionalized, so I haven't been able to call him, but they did let me use the Internet today, so I wanted to share with you all what a fabulous friend I have in Bill! Here are some of my favorite emails we've exchanged!

```
From: Aaaaaaron
Date: Jan 23, 2006 1:09 PM

Hey Bill,

It was nice talking to you today.  I hope I get out to NYC sometime
soon so we can hang out.

aaron
```

```
From: Bill Dawes
Date: Jan 23, 2006 8:14 PM

Aaron, you're kind of creeping me out. Please stop calling me. Bill.
```

```
From: Aaaaaaron
Date: Jan 24, 2006 3:22 AM

Hey Bill,

I'm glad you were up when I called.  It sure was nice of you to give me
your number.  It's great that I can call you whenever I want.

And you can call me.

But I'm sure you're busy.

That's okay, because I don't mind being the one that calls.  I think
I'll call right now and see what you're up to.

aaron
```

From: Bill Dawes
Date: Jan 24, 2006 3:45 PM

Seriously, Aaron, you've got to stop calling me. I'm sure you're just
lonely or something but I don't appreciate it. I only gave you my
number because I thought you were sane. Don't ever call me again. Bill.

From: Aaaaaaron
Date: Jan 25, 2006 4:37 AM

So, what's up with your cell phone? Did you forget to pay the bill?
Ha ha. Did "Bill" forget to pay the "bill"? Ha ha. I bet you get
that all the time when you don't pay your cell phone bill.

I haven't tried calling you for an hour or so--maybe you've paid it by
now. I'm going to try.

From: Bill Dawes
Date: Jan 25, 2006 9:27 AM

Don't ever send me a message again. I've already had to change my cell
number because of you. Just leave me alone. Bill.

From: Aaaaaaron
Date: Jan 25, 2006 9:36 AM

I'm lucky to have a friend like you--you respond to my messages as if
you really KNOW me, you know? I'm sure you're incredibly busy with
your "comedy" and everything and yet you still take time to write me
now and then. I appreciate that.

So, I came up with a funny skit you should do in your standup. What
made me think of it is that it's called "standup," get it? You should
come out on stage with a chair and do "sit-down" comedy, get it? That
would be pretty funny, huh? You can do your show that way when I come
to visit!

From: Bill Dawes
Date: Jan 26, 2006 8:58 AM

I don't know how you got my new cell number but DO NOT EVER CALL IT
AGAIN.

Seriously, I will hurt you. Bill.

From: Aaaaaaron
Date: Jan 26, 2006 9:12 AM

You're so funny, Bill. It must be nice being funny. Plus, you've got
those boyish good looks. I bet it's no problem getting laid, huh?
When I come out to New York, we will totally hang out and you can get
me laid, right? I mean, I don't care if we have to share, you know?

So, your mom was pretty surprised to hear you were trapped in a mine
shaft and that I needed to call your cell phone to track your precise
location, since that's what I told her. She seemed to take the news
well, but I tried to be as understanding as possible, considering.

I like your mom. She seems nice. I'll be honest- she's not really my
type, but I've learned not to pass judgment too early.

I keep calling you and getting your voice mail for some reason. You
must be extra busy. Did you get a part in a movie again? That would
be nice. Maybe I'll come out for the premiere! Wouldn't that be cool,
two cool guys stepping out of the limo with all the cameras flashing
and everything--there I'd be, right by your side!

From: Bill Dawes
Date: Jan 26, 2006 11:23 AM

Fuck you. Now you've done it.

From: Aaaaaaron
Date: Feb 6, 2006 8:34 AM

Hey Bill,

Sorry it's been a while, but I've been institutionalized. And before
that, someone jumped me in a dark alley and beat the crap out of me.

I *know* it was Jennifer Aniston. Tell someone they have the perkiest
nipples once and they think you're cute, but tell her 296 times and she
freaks out. What a world.... So anyway, strangely enough a van pulled
up and put the white jacket on me right after I was beaten up.   It's
almost like they knew exactly where to find me.

So, it took me a while to convince them that if I didn't email you your
medication schedule, you would die painfully. I miss calling you every
ten minutes. It's going to be difficult not being able to stay in
touch, but fortunately I printed up all 379 images that Google's image
search found under your name. Of course, some of them weren't you but
I still THINK of you when I see them and that's what counts, right?

Don't get too lonely! I'll think of you often,

aaron

This blog was especially fun to do. BiBi
Cambridge left a phone number on the Bill Dawes
blog, implying that I should stalk her instead, but
when I called the number, all I got was an error
message.

She finally admitted through online
messages that it wasn't her real number, which
gave me the idea to do this blog. She is every bit
as good of a sport as Bill for letting me print it.

I thought the ending was a little over the
top, but since I couldn't figure out another way to
end it, I posted it, anyway. This happens to me a
lot: I worry about being a little too inappropriate,
then discover that my readership is much more
accepting (less prudish?) than I am.

My dirty phone conversation with BiBi Cambridge

Remember that blog I wrote about calling Bill Dawes all the time? Well, on that blog, BiBi Cambridge posted a comment containing her phone number and it would have been an insult to the fine lady if I didn't call her! Naturally, things got dirty quickly and I've decided to share the details here:

BIBI CAMBRIDGE: Uptown Laundry.

AARON DIETZ: BiBi, hey! What's up?!

CAMBRIDGE: This is Uptown Laundry.

DIETZ: Yeah, baby! I got some dirty laundry for ya'!

CAMBRIDGE: Sir, no one works here named—

DIETZ: Ooo! Sir, huh? That must make me a knight! Sir Aaron to the rescue!

CAMBRIDGE: Sir, you've dialed th—

DIETZ: That's right. You BETTER call me 'sir.' I'm a knight, after all. You knighted me. Don't make me use my sword.

CAMBRIDGE: Sir, you've got the wrong—

DIETZ: Oh, so you WANT me to use my sword? You want me to get my sword out? I'll be honest—it's more like a small dagger or a pocketknife.

CAMBRIDGE: Sir, you've—

DIETZ: I've learned it's better to be straightforward about the length of the blade—less disappointment later, you see.

CAMBRIDGE: Sir—

DIETZ: But it's still sharp, made of steel and all that. Are you naked yet?

CAMBRIDGE: Sir, this is Uptown Laundry.

DIETZ: Yeah, baby! You're taking me to Uptown, all right! It's up and ready, baby! Are you excited?

CAMBRIDGE: I said this is Uptown Laundry.

DIETZ: Yeah, baby! We're gonna' make dirty laundry together! I'm gonna' make dirty laundry with BiBi Cambridge!

CAMBRIDGE: Sir, there is no BiBi Cambridge at this number.

DIETZ: I know there isn't, darling. You're so beside yourself with passion for my steel that you don't know who you are anymore!

CAMBRIDGE: Bloody hell.

DIETZ: Oh my, that's REALLY dirty! Don't worry, baby—I know who you are. You're BiBi, baby—a hot female ready for a sexual telecommunication with Sir Aaron!

CAMBRIDGE: Sir, I'm not even a woman.

DIETZ: BiBi, baby, you can't fool me. Your low voice might have turned away knights of lesser courage but I can recognize a damsel in desperation when I hear one.

CAMBRIDGE: [CLICK]

DIETZ: Let's go, baby! Are you ready to taste my steel? Can you taste my steel over the phone? Here, let me taste it for you.

[PAUSE]

DIETZ (CONTINUED): BiBi? BiBi, baby—I think I hurt myself. BiBi, could you call me an ambulance please? I can't move my fingers now. BiBi? Can you hear me?

Ever Wonder About My Penis?

Me too.

Sometimes, I'll write a manic rant that is entertaining enough to post.

Naturally, I didn't go out and impregnate anyone. I'm pretty sure I stayed in that night. I probably did some reading.

Hospitals of Seattle—
you will be busy 9 months from tonight!

Because tonight is my night. I'm going to impregnate every woman I can get my hands on. And I can get my hands on a lot of women, let me tell you.

You must be wondering: with what, pray tell, am I going to impregnate half of Seattle?

With MyCock. It's beautiful. Yes, it's a bit small, but it's chock full of vitamins and minerals. No, I won't give away the recipe. And quit asking.

I feel bad for all the maternity wards, but it simply must be done. I can no longer hold back for the sake of doctors and nurses in this area. At least I gave you fair warning. You have 9 months to plan.

I am constantly befriending females, which
aggravates other men sometimes. They either
think I'm gay or really wussy, because obviously
(from their point of view), the only reason to be
friends with a girl is so that you can someday have
sex with them. I don't understand this concept,
but there is much I don't understand about
traditional masculinity.

I'm sorry, female friends—
I was unaware of how badly I was treating you

I have been informed that a heterosexual male cannot have fulfilling friendships with females unless he is currently having sex with them.

Thus, female friends of mine, we must commence at once. I can't afford to lose friends and there is no point in delaying what people have informed me is inevitable: we must get it on.

I apologize for not knowing about these rules. You must have thought there was something wrong because I had not initiated the sex act with you. Or, you thought I was gay. In any case, it wasn't you. It was me. It was my ignorance of the social mores of our time. I won't make this mistake again.

The Redhead drafted this plan over coffee after I
admitted to having a crush.

Oddly enough, I did follow the plan,
though I had no intention of doing so. One day, I
happened to notice that the girl I had a crush on
seemed a bit down, so naturally, I asked if she was
okay. I hope she really was.

Yes, the pun in the title was intentional.

The Best Laid Plans of The Redhead

The Redhead's Plan For Me To Get a Girlfriend:

    1. Be friendly around girl I have crush on.
    2. Notice when she is having a bad day.
    3. Say, "Are you okay?"

Theoretical Result: She realizes I'm a sensitive, kind man and decides she wants me. She gives me anal sex and we live happily ever after.

My Execution of The Redhead's Plan:

    1. I am friendly around the girl I have a crush on.
    2. I notice she is having a bad day.
    3. I say, "Are you okay?"

Actual Result: She says, "What? Yeah. Why?" and has no idea what I am talking about. I find out that she is a lesbian and try to ignore the fact that I get warmer whenever she says my name.

I think just about everyone has been on one
side or the other of a conversation like this.
The idea that somehow you will beat the odds,
that somehow *everyone* will beat the odds is
completely ludicrous, yet this conversation keeps
happening.

If you've found that special someone,
more power to you. But don't tell the rest of the
population it will definitely happen. That's insane.
Everyone has their own path. Some people's
paths will be lonelier than others.

For All Who Haven't Found Their Special Someone

I had the following conversation with a friend the other day:

Friend: "I will never find someone special."

Me: "Oh, don't get too disheartened. It could happen."

Friend: "Yeah, right."

Me: "I was just like you. I had all but given up on love. I had thought it would never happen. Yet, I found this amazing girlfriend. And my whole life is incredible now."

Friend: "Harumph."

Me: "But I know how it feels. And I'm not going to tell you that it WILL happen for certain. In fact, It's pretty unlikely. I'm not one of those people who, just because it happened to them, will ignore all statistical probability and tell you that it definitely will happen to you. It probably won't."

Friend: "Yeah, you're right."

Me: "I know I am."

Then, my friend went off and devoted himself to scientific research and saved the world by developing a cure to an as yet unknown disease (whew!).

Except, I never had this conversation, because "it" never happened to me either. To make matters worse, it's highly doubtful I will be able to save the world. Yes, the probability of either of these two events happening to me is pretty slim. I'm not going to tell you otherwise.

I wish I could say where I got the inspiration for
this blog because I'd go back there and get more
if I could. This just came out one day. I loved the
concept of having a character that spoke English
that was understood by the reader, but not by the
narrator.

      Someone pointed out that Czechoslovakia
no longer exists, which I was aware of. I went
with Czechoslovakia because it's the first thing
that popped into my head that was a long enough
word that would work for the piece. That's
all. And besides, they make some great potato
dishes—I'd like everyone to remember that.

So, I got a roommate

A Russian bride, to be more exact. We've been learning each other's languages when there's time (and let's face it—I don't have any time so it's all up to her, you know). She's terrified of the city because she grew up in Siberia, or some other place, I don't know. So she never leaves the house (did I say house? I meant studio apartment).

Yeah, so except today—I woke up from sleeping in late and she says to me, "I go outside." And I'm like, "Sure, baby, when I get around to it, I'll take you outside." Ha ha! Little did I know, she was trying to tell me that she had already gone outside. It was so cute that she said, "I go outside," and everything and she showed me the receipt she got from buying a muffin at the coffee shop. Oh, I had a good laugh about that one. And then I took away her keys.

Sometimes she speaks to me in Russian and I'm like, "Baby, you know I don't have no time to learn the Russian just yet!" But no, she just keeps shouting things like, "Tern dounthe tea vee!" or "Iyam go wing too bye uh guhnand shoo tyu." I mean seriously, does she think I'm going to pick up the language just because she repeats the words over and over?!

I can hear her now, in the other room, shouting at me even as I watch the NASCAR over the clutter of her making so much noise doing the dishes. "Iyate jif gore din!" Where does she get this stuff? Does the Russian language really have so many words?

Now, she's saying, "Iyam nut rush in iyam check is love ockeean." What the heck?! Hey, I'm just writin' down what the words sound like. Maybe you Rooskie readers can do some translatin'....

I liked the narrator's character so much I decided to turn this into a trilogy. Unfortunately, the next two installments are very much like most sequels: they never quite capture the energy of the first one. In this case, it's primarily because there is no longer a Czechoslovakian bride in the story but that was a conscious decision. I just couldn't bring myself to run that joke into the ground.

In any case, why is it that they make those refrigerator wrinkles so hard to clean? I'm still annoyed by this.

It were men that done this!

Yes, the little Russian gal has run off, leaving me high and dry. I'm not worried, though, since there isn't nobody that can understand a word of her Rooskie-speak anyway.

But...that's not what I'm here to chat about. No sir. Since it'll be another couple months before I can afford another Russian bride, I got it in my head to do some cleaning and well, I ain't never cleaned before, so I figured I'd start on the tall stuff first. It was that idea that led me to believe the entire world of design has gone astray.

You see, my frigerator got all dusty on top and I discovered that, because of the little wrinkly design of the casing, the dust just don't never come out of the wrinkles. It won't never be clean, no matter what chemical I employ.

Then I thought to myself, "It were men that designed this!" And they probably didn't know what hell they created because they hain't never cleaned the top of a frigerator before!

This event has forced me to question my pride in my own manhood. Yep, men done ruined my day. Maybe my whole entire week.

I wanted to take the narrator and break him down
a little bit, and maybe I was even thinking I'd leave
the series open in case I got more inspiration to
continue it. As it stands, the series is halted at a
trilogy, though I suppose it's always possible that
the "Russian" bride could return in the future....

Oh, Russian Lady, Why Did You Ever Leave Me?

I miss her, folks. And I never even learned her Rooskie name.

And since I've had to get used to doing everything myself, I've gained a newly found respect for all the things the lil' lady did for me.

For one, there is suddenly a problem with the layout of the apartment. Beer goes in the frigerator, yet I recline on the sofa. I tried moving the sofa next to the frigerator, but then I couldn't see the TV. So then I moved the TV into the kitchen and got settled again when I realized—I had forgotten the remote! Well, it was always the Russian lady that done brought me the remote! Yes, it's about made me cry not having her around.

Also, I always thought that the cuts on her wrists and hands were pathetic cries for attention, but I realize now—that's just what happens when you don't have a can opener and refuse to get one and have to open cans with a giant meat cleaver.

Well, Russian lady, I plunked down two bits for a can opener at a garage sale. If you ever learn English and happen to read this, please come back!

I remember scratching this out on the bus one
night, a little drunk. I thought it was insanely
funny at the time, woke up the next day and *still*
thought it was...well...funny enough to print,
anyway.

Oh, Tomato Soup, Why Did You Ever Leave Me?

I know I didn't treat you well. I had a multitude of tasty goods while I kept you in the cupboard. I only came to you when I was in need, when I was starving and out of options.

Even then, while warming you up, I was inattentive—I let a film develop on the surface that had to be dealt with during each new stirring of affection.

And then I...oh...I'm starting to remember....

You never left me. I devoured you. I scooped out your insides, every part of you that was good and useful, then absorbed what I wanted, made it a part of me. What I didn't use, I ejected into the sewer.

In the end, all that was left of you was a cold metal shell. And I made sure you were headed to a place that would crush you completely, then re-mold you and send you back out into the world only to relive the experience all over again.

I'm so sorry.

I despise poorly written directions. Telling someone how they could do things differently after they've already done it is just not the best way togive instructions.

June 26, 2005

Thanks, it would have been helpful to know that before I cooked the entire fucking pizza

What is wrong with people that write instructions for cooking crappy processed food out of a box?

I followed the directions in order, you see. I pre-heated the oven to 400 degrees. I put the pizza in for 16-18 minutes. I took it out. Then I read the final instruction: "For a softer crust, bake the fucking pizza at a different fucking temperature for a different fucking amount of time" (some words added or entirely changed to make a point).

It's like high altitude instructions that you always find at the bottom of the list of directions—I've already baked your "Potatoes Au Gratin" and *now* you tell me that if I live in Colorado, I should have altered how much water I used?

Thank you. Thank you very much. You've been most helpful.

I post blogs in various places, wherever readers will read them, for the most part. Usually, I'll post a copy of a blog on each of the several blogging sites I use.

This blog, however, I was never super sure of, so I only posted it in one place. It didn't quite have that "togetherness" that I like a blog to have, that concise, unified purpose that most any piece of good writing offers. But there are exceptions to all rules (including that one) and when I was compiling the book, I liked this one more than I had when I posted it online, so I included it.

Hi. I am a fucktard.
Please give my life meaning now.

I go to the grocery store. A young woman there says to her young woman friend, "I mean what does that mean? Great Northern Bean? There's no bean named Great Northern Bean."

She was lovely but no, she will never mate with me.

Walking home I hear the sound of an animal in pain, screeching behind me. But no, I discover it is a human, screeching at seeing her friend a half block away. If I had known it was a human I would not have turned around.

I think it's easy to see how the previous blog inspired this one. The previous blog had something in it that I wanted to focus on and bring out in a better way.

This *is* a real problem. I make light of it here by blaming it on sorority girls, but the truth is that a lot of people squeal for no reason and those of us with heroes hiding in our hearts look out our windows, just in case there should be an emergency we need to attend to. Immediately, we are disheartened for having wasted our time.

This is why there are no more heroes

It is because every time they hear what sounds like a distress call,
it turns out to be a sorority girl squealing for no apparent reason.

Someone, please teach them other ways of expressing themselves.

I have had so many peanut butter jelly sandwiches in my life that now when I eat them, it is a struggle not to wretch. It's a shame, too, because they taste good. This blog has several things going on:

One. Words like, "once," "so," and "okay," really start off a blog with a bang. I would often use them in the titles of pieces, just because for some reason, it sounds funnier when you start your title that way. For this piece, I went all out and used all three at the beginning of the first sentence.

Two. I use the phrase, "What a world," in this blog. I love that phrase. If you've been paying attention, you already know that this isn't the first time it appears in this book. You probably know where it's from, too.

Three. This is one of the "it didn't happen that way" series of blogs. I tell a story, then at the end I tell you how it wasn't quite like that.

And that's when I discovered vital information about soaking peanut butter knives

Okay, so, once I was very poor. Therefore, I had peanut butter and jelly sandwiches every day for lunch. All right, since I could afford the jelly, maybe I was only *somewhat* poor, but that's off the subject.

Since I had peanut butter and jelly sandwiches every day, every day I would have to wash a knife that I had used to spread the peanut butter. This was the bane of my existence. Oh, how I hated to wash that peanut butter knife. Peanut butter just does not wash off of stuff that easy (as some of you fetishists know).

However, then I got some money so I didn't have to eat peanut butter anymore, so I didn't have any peanut butter knives to wash. How glorious that life was!

But now I've moved to Seattle and am unemployed and thus—I am poor, so I'm back to peanut butter and jelly sandwiches.

Anyway, by accident, a knife that I used to spread the peanut butter was placed in a plate in the sink. The plate has a pseudo-Asian design and thus it is almost a bowl and is therefore capable of containing water. Hence, my use of the sink caused the knife to be soaked for a few minutes before I washed it.

Wow, what a difference! That knife was the easiest peanut butter knife I've ever washed.

And to think that I can still be learning things at age 30! Here I was, thinking my education was over. What a world!

Except that I'm actually using almond butter instead of peanut butter and I'm not really into sweets anymore so I skip the jelly. Oh, and also, I don't use bread; I just spread the almond butter on a tortilla and eat it like a rollup.

So this may not have anything to do with peanut butter knives at all.

There is some truth in this one, but not much.
I really did have a very good orange port and I
didn't have a corkscrew when I first moved in. I
even had a downstairs neighbor named Tim, who
lived with his girlfriend, but for some reason I
never went down to hang out with them in all of
the two months that I lived there. They seemed
very nice, though. They didn't seem like the type
of people that would steal a corkscrew, anyway.

And this piece has a surprise ending

So, this guy moved in above me and he's friendly enough and one night I invited him in for a beer.

But then he brought down this bottle of orange port and told me and my girlfriend how it was so special because it was orange and all. And it did look kind of special, since it was orange-colored.

Anyway, we were like, "Oh man, that'd be nice but we don't have a corkscrew."

He says, "No problem," and he goes and gets a corkscrew from upstairs.

When he comes back he tells us this pitiful story about how he and his sister wanted to open the port the night she helped him move in, but he didn't have a corkscrew. So then, he went and bought a corkscrew but not 'til after his sister left, and since he doesn't know anyone in town, he didn't have anyone to share the port with, so he never opened it. He was very pleased to have finally gotten the opportunity to share the port.

We had a decent time, drinking the port and talking about guitar, and then he went back upstairs. It was then that my girlfriend and I made fun of him for being so uptight. Then we laughed at how pitiful he was that he was so proud of his corkscrew.

"That's so sad that he didn't have anyone to share the port with," said my girlfriend, seriously.

And then we both cracked up. It was truly hilarious.

So wait, the story continues. The next morning, we realized that he left his corkscrew here and we decided to keep it, since we didn't have one. Later that day, he stopped by and knocked and my girlfriend and I knew why he had come—he wanted that corkscrew back. So we pretended not to be home, even though we had music turned up pretty loud.

And he has since knocked several times and even said, "I know you're in there! Can I have my corkscrew back?"

And we have had quite a good laugh at his expense, let me tell you.

And the point of this story is that I was not the narrator, but rather the guy upstairs and I want my corkscrew back, so give me back my corkscrew, Tim!

I'm not going to comment on this piece, except
to say that duct tape is pretty cool. I recommend
having some around for whatever reason, just in
case.

Once, I broke a bed at a hotel

Only, not with a girl, with three guys. For some of you, this may not come as a surprise.

But anyway, we were there as friends, for a convention, and nobody got it on, okay?

My friend, Jimbo, decided it would be a good idea to run in from the hallway, jump off one bed, fly through the room and land on the other bed. It was pretty fun! One can really propel themselves through the air, you know?

Well, after a few hours of that, we took to streaking in the hallway, since that was where our boom box was playing the music the loudest. But Jimbo kept leaping off the bed 'cause he just preferred that.

After a while, I saw him walk sheepishly out of the room. He said, "Guys, I broke the bed."

And he was right. The bed was resting at an angle now, one leg having been broken clean off.

And what do you know if ToastMan didn't have a plan! Because he just went out to his truck, grabbed the duct tape and taped that leg back. As good as new!

And in this story I was actually Jimbo, and Jimbo was me, and ToastMan was ToastMan. The duct tape was duct tape. Brian doesn't appear in this story. Nor does Frank. Or anyone else until the very end.

So you see, it was me that broke the bed.

This really happened. I was being a little
melodramatic and down on myself one day over
coffee, and somehow this woman developed this
theory that I was impotent. Strange.

Once, A Woman Thought I Was Impotent

This came about because we were discussing life one time and she asked me why I was sad.

I don't remember what I said, exactly, but it was something vague, like, "Life...has been very difficult for me." (Yes, I even paused like that because I like attention.)

I was meaning because of my chronic depression, because of my view of life as a series of mechanical movements—like a game that you've figured out all of the rules to and thus discovered: there is no point to the game!

But she took this to mean I was impotent.

It was a simple mistake, really. They are pretty much the same thing.

I'm not going to tell you, even in the commentary,
how this little problem was solved, mostly because
the real-life solution was more boring than
anything you might imagine.

Once, a girl accidentally implied
that I should get naked

Some years ago, my roommate locked me out of my dorm as I was taking a shower. I came back to the room in nothing but my boxers and couldn't get in, so I set my towel and my bucket o' shower stuff by the door and went to go get a spare key.

To get a spare key, I had to leave the building, cross a courtyard and a parking lot and go into an entirely different building.

There I talked to a girl behind a desk and she said that they do have spare keys. Hooray! Then she said, "We make you leave something with us, though, so you remember to return the key."

"Okay," I said. And I looked down at my bare feet and my naked legs and my boxers and my bare chest. "What would you have me leave?" I asked.

I'm not going to get into how *that* little quandary was solved.

I watched Jamal's show when he held his "Pick My New Name" contest. I guess I sort of felt sorry for him, because I figured he would probably get a bunch of bad names to choose from, yet he seemed crazy enough to go through with it and actually change his name to the best entry.

I knew his name was Jamal, so I sent in my entry of "Jamal," just so he'd have it as an option in case he didn't like any of the others.

And I won the contest! Bonus!

I decided a man's name once

Once upon a time, a man had a naming contest. He changed his name often and decided, this time, to offer people everywhere (as long as they happened to watch his public access television show) the opportunity to name him.

I somehow sensed that I had the innate ability to name this one man, if not others. So, I thought and thought for seconds upon seconds. Finally, I came up with the perfect name. I knew it was perfect because the heavens opened up before me and said so. And by that, I mean I wrote it down on a 3 X 5 inch notecard, which definitely gave it a sense of officiality.

I sent in my winning entry, saying on the notecard, "I think you should be Jamal."

And my winning entry was noted on pre-recorded public access television and my name was mentioned and everything and I was a big star.

This really did happen to me. I was definitely
feeling down that day. The last thing I wanted was
some dude trying to cheer me up.

And it's not that I didn't want to be happy.
It's that there was something else going on in
this interaction. He saw someone in a state of
mind that he didn't like and attempted to make
me conform to what he wanted. His intentions
may have been pure (as in, he may have earnestly
wanted to cheer me up), but I definitely had a
problem with the way he went about it.

So he said, "Come on, it's never *that* bad!"
And as I walked past him, after giving him the
weak smile, I said, not to anyone in particular,
but loud enough that he may have heard it,
"Sometimes it is." Because, really, sometimes it is.

A Jerkface Harassed Me This One Time

Once, I was walking and I was depressed, so naturally I had a depressed look on my face.

I walked by this guy and he stopped me and said, "Come on, it's never THAT bad!"

So I gave him a weak smile so he would leave me alone.

It was really at that moment that I learned I need to keep a positive face on at all times—not because I think it spreads goodwill and makes the world better and all that, but because otherwise jerkfaces will harass you.

It's pretty amazing how many people don't know
what time it is. You'd think people that needed
to know this information would carry a watch
or something, but that's not how it works. They
just wander around timelessly and expect people
to walk by and tell them the time whenever they
need to know. I guess if they can get by that way,
more power to them (even though I am often
annoyed at being asked).

But jeez, the guy that asked me
where Aloha Street was—I had moved to the
neighborhood only a month or two before and he
practically freaked out when I didn't know. He
said something like, "Call yourself a local?"

Hey, I knew where I was. People. You
have to laugh at them. Otherwise, you become
one.

The answer is NO,
nobody really knows what time it is

This is obviously true, because they freaking keep asking me! What is wrong with people? If it's really that important to know what time it is, shouldn't you be wearing a watch? You weirdos ask me every time I leave the house! It's pathetic.

Oh, and to the rude individual I met outside my apartment building the other day, I know where Aloha Street is now and you were nowhere near it.

This is, once more, an ode to people that ask me questions while I'm out walking around. I don't own a car and I like to walk, so this happens almost daily.

It boggles the mind that people are out there without any idea where they are or what time it is. How do they survive? I mean, do they just say, "I think I'll go to the courthouse now!" and walk out the door without any idea how to get there?

Maybe it's just me. Maybe I have this look on my face that makes people think I have the answer. Oddly enough, usually I do.

Public Service Announcement: I Am Not A Map

Maps. They were invented long ago, no matter what continent you are talking about. They are usually graphic representations of geographic locations—pretty handy if you want to know how to get from Point A to Point B. I suggest you pick one up if you are unfamiliar with where you are going. These days, you can even look one up on the Internet. Try mapquest.com. The point is: maps can help you.

Here is what a map isn't, just in case you still don't understand. A map is not a six foot tall, short haired, skinny, neurotic, geeky weirdo who walks all over the place because he has no car.

Thanks for listening. I was noticing that a lot of you were confused about this. Maybe now you can get where you're going without pestering me.

I can't stand people that walk together as if they cannot be separated. Often, they can't even get out of your way when you approach them on the sidewalk. It shows how thoughtless and self-absorbed people can be. Share the sidewalk. It's a small world.

So, how does it feel to make out with your sibling?

Is it hot? Or is it weird?

What's that? What do I mean, you say? You two are going out, aren't you? I thought so. You were giving off that, "We're going steady," vibe. So, yeah, how does it feel then, making out with your sibling and all?

Oh, I'm sorry, you're not conjoined twins? My mistake. I made that assumption based on the way you were unable to separate in order to allow people to pass you on the sidewalk.

You must be royalty, then! Boy, is my face red. If I'd have only known, I would have thrown myself into the street as you approached, instead of trying to rudely maintain my position on the sidewalk as I passed you.

Next time, I promise a bow, if the cars don't hit me first.

This really happened to me. What this old man said while I was walking by was so absolutely brilliant I had to share it with everyone. He had such a nice, gravelly voice, too.

The Secret of Existence

This afternoon I walked by an old man talking to an opportunist at a yard sale.

"Without coffee, I can't even exist," he said with a Bukowski voice.

It suddenly struck me that this is why I'm so tired all the time: existence. As the old man pointed out, it takes a strain on your body and soul. Without coffee, he can't even do it!

Sadly, I never thought of the fact that we are expending energy just to materialize physically in this world. But as luck would have it, coffee was discovered by sheepherders well over a thousand years ago, allowing many of us to exist here today.

Moral: Be thankful for sheep.

My reality is not incredibly sound. Is yours?

Verisimilitude

INTERVIEWER: Do you use a lot of material from your own life in your writing?

AARON DIETZ: Of course. It's unavoidable. Like the other day, I was at the bank, right? And I was going to deposit a check and I walked up to the teller, right?

INTERVIEWER: Sure.

DIETZ: But then this guy comes in with a mask on and he points a gun all over and he totally robs the bank right there!

INTERVIEWER: Wow. That must have been very frightening.

DIETZ: Well, not really. I mean, afterward it is. But during, you kind of think about other stuff, because you don't have time to be afraid, you know? Like, I was thinking stuff like, 'Okay, don't make any sudden movements.' 'I hope he doesn't want to shoot anybody.' 'I should have gone to the bank yesterday,' that kind of thing.

INTERVIEWER: Well, you made it out in one piece, apparently.

DIETZ: Yeah, nobody was hurt, and I heard they caught the guy a few hours later.

INTERVIEWER: That must have given you some great material to write about.

DIETZ: Oh yeah, definitely. It's like I was saying, I was about to deposit that check and I thought, 'What if I were a sheep trying to open a bank account?' you know? And then I was like, 'But what if I wasn't even from the same time,' you know? Like, a time traveling sheep. And then I was like, 'That'd be sweet!'

This next one is one of my all time favorites. I just love the absurdity of time travel in fiction.   Why does it seem natural to assume that if we travel through time, the Earth will be in the exact same place as it was in the time we just left?

These time travelers are completely ignoring the fact that the Earth moves. Michael J. Fox's character in *Back to the Future* would have blasted back to the fifties to a time where the Earth was not at all in the same exact place as it was when he left. Most likely, he would have frozen to death in seconds as he suddenly appeared in the middle of space, in the near-zero temperature of the cold void.

I will concede, however, that H.G. Wells' apparatus might potentially move *with* the Earth, since the way it works makes use of a continuous stream of travel, rather than an instantaneous burst into the next time frame.

Oh yeah—I also like this blog because it contains the word, "SHABAM," which I find to be a hilarious word.

The call back to a famous *Star Trek* episode was intentional.

One more note: "dufus" is an accepted spelling of the word, "doofus." Some people don't know this. There may be *other* misspellings in this book, but that word is okay.

The Trouble With Time Travel

All right. Say you've figured out how to travel through time, right? And you build this awesome machine that can do it, if only you pedal these wheels and sit in a certain chair, like an exercise bike, right? You might have to twiddle some knobs or something, too.

Or, maybe you are in a DeLorean, cruising toward the speed of 55mph. That's all you have to do, because you've done the hard part. You've figured out how to travel through time and now you're doing it.

SHABAM! You've traveled through time.

Congratulations. You are now in the middle of space. You are instantly frozen from the frigid near absolute zero temperatures of the great abyss. You are dead.

Oh, I'm sorry—did you think the Earth would be in the same exact place in this new time you've traveled to? I guess you're not so smart after all!

Problem number 1: The Earth is spinning about its axis. Thus, when you time travel back to 1955, you do not end up on the same exact road you were on—you end up in France, or in the middle of the ocean! Dufus! But that's if this is the ONLY problem you are facing. And it isn't.

Problem number 2: The Earth is moving about the sun. If this were the only other problem you were facing, you could just time travel back to the same day of the year, at precisely the same time and you'd mostly be okay. But no! There are more problems!

Problem number 3: The speed of the sun. The sun is roaming about our galaxy at a speed of over 200 kilometers per second. In short, your little road in 1955 is way the hell far away from you by now. Stupid, stupid, stupid!

And our galaxy is also traveling about the universe, etc! So basically, you haven't solved much of anything, have you? You're a failure! This is precisely why the other scientists are laughing at you! They *want* you to try out your new time travel machine. Heheh. Do it. Yeh, go ahead.

A lot of my writing explores the concept of not fitting in, whether it be not being from this time period, or not having the right shoes to be in the right group. It's not intentional. That's just what comes out of me.

I'm A Lesbian!

So I'm having pancakes with three friends: C-Dawg, a lesbian, and a guy who doesn't appear in this story.

C-Dawg is all talking about lesbians and shoes because a friend of hers called wondering what shoes to wear to C-Dawg's party 'cause she only had lesbian shoes.

"She says it's some sort of lesbian code so that other lesbians can tell you're a lesbian," C-Dawg explains.

And the lesbian eating with us confirms this.

I am like, "Well, damn, I want lesbian shoes if that's all it takes."

The lesbian looks at my shoes and says, "You've got 'em."

And everything suddenly makes sense to me: the reason why I feel so gay all the time while being into women.... I'm a lesbian! It is so simple!

But then she takes a closer look and adds, "Sort of," which did put a slight damper on things.

This was tough. A reader named Randy sent in a list of 25 blog topics because I told him I would write a blog on whatever topic he chose. Having 25 options was a bonus. But since picking one didn't seem challenging enough, I decided to try and string them together into one continuous story. I even kept them in the order that he gave them.

The topics he gave are listed right along with the story, so that you can follow how I incorporated each topic into the narrative.

I wish there were a book called *A Technical Manual for Random Things*. I'd buy it, or at least check it out from the library.

See How My Big Toe Dances!

:: Topic 1 :: My big toe and how it dances

Fred reclined in the recliner, watching his big toe and how his big toe danced in the air.

"See my big toe! See how it dances!" he said.

"It dances like a cheeseburger," said George.

"You're just hungry."

:: Topic 2 :: Where to eat a cheeseburger

"Even so, where's the best place to eat a cheeseburger around here?"

"Nowhere. I'm vegetarian," said Fred.

"Vegetarians suck," George said. He looked down. "This carpet sucks."

:: Topic 3 :: Cool facts about carpet and other flooring

"A dog's ass supposedly leaves no bacteria behind on the carpet."[1]

"I don't believe that for a second."

"I suppose it would be true about other flooring, as well," Fred said. He picked up a book called *A Technical Manual for Random Things*, then dropped it suddenly.

"Ow," he said. "Paper cuts suck."

"I'll tell you what sucks: paper. It should be outlawed."

:: Topic 4 :: Why I still use paper

"Still, at least it doesn't radiate you, like computers," said Fred. "That's why I still use paper."

"Damn. Your finger's bleeding, dude."

:: Topic 5 :: Does it hurt when you type?

"Yeah. That's going to hurt when I type."

He put his finger in his mouth and picked up the book again with his other hand. Leafing through it, he paused to read a random entry.

:: Topic 6 :: Everything a MySpacer needs to know about HTML, cake, and binder clips

"A MySpacer need know nothing of HTML, though some rudimentary knowledge of how to post images will expand their 'witty repertoire' when they want to comment on people's profiles. As for cake, any good MySpacer knows that the best knowledge of cake comes from Psmith-Wainscotting's This Week In Cake.[2] MySpacers AND real human beings would be well-served to know that binder clips, especially of the large variety, are quite useful for keeping an open bag of chips as fresh as possible. Simply fold over the top of the bag, and clip the top with the binder clip."

"I hate that book," said George.

Flipping to a new page, Fred continued to read.

:: Topic 7 :: When time slows down and where

"Time slows down approximately when and where matter and space begin divorce proceedings. Attorneys are usually brought in to help with negotiations, but in this case, attorneys are not called by that name. In these matters, they are usually referred to as drugs."

Fred turned another page.

:: Topic 8 :: A brief lesson on septic systems and the Puget Sound

"How about this, George? Says here that poorly maintained septic systems can actually be responsible for polluting the Puget Sound."[3]

"Bloody environmentalists. They'll get us all killed one of these days. Read about something else, will ya'?"

:: Topic 9 :: Where does the bread go when you make toast?

"Here's something: *Bread undergoes transportation to the toasting realm through the use of toastporters, the red strips of heat residing in all true toasters. While the bread is in the toasting realm, it begins its physical transformation into toast. Sometimes, the toaster doesn't quite have time to—"*

"Good grief. Who cares about freakin' toast?!"

:: Topic 10 :: How to jump

"Would you rather I read about how to jump?"

"No. Just shut up."

"It sounds quite simple. You might learn something. It'd be like a first kiss, maybe."

:: Topic 11 :: The first evergreen tree I ever kissed

"My first kiss was with a tree."

"Oh. What kind of tree?"

"An evergreen."

"Wow. How was it?"

"Awful. I accidentally ate a lady bug."

:: Topic 12 :: Lady bugs: aren't they neat?

"Wow. That's pretty neat. Aren't lady bugs neat?"

"Not when you swallow them and they fly back up out of your mouth."

Fred sighed. "Then what happened?"

:: Topic 13 :: Rows and rows of corn

"I freaked out. I thought that kissing produced lady bugs and I freaked out, ran out of the forest through rows and rows of corn, and I wound up tripping over the cat and smashing my face on a rock."

:: Topic 14 :: How to run over a cat

"You can never run over a cat when you want to. The trick is to not want to."

"It's a nice day to go for a walk and get something to eat, don't you think?"

"You're just changing the subject because we have to move on to the next topic that Randy suggested."

:: Topic 15 :: Puffy clouds and their shapes

"No, it's really a nice day. Look: there are all these nice puffy clouds everywhere. Some of them even have nice shapes. Like those—they look like boobs. And those over there...they look like...boobs."

Fred looked out the window. "Yeah, I'll give you that. Boobs. Everywhere."

"And besides, I'm hungry. I could eat a plastic trash bag."

:: Topic 16 :: Plastic trash bags and why not to eat them

"Oh, I wouldn't recommend that. If you don't suffocate first, you'll probably die of cancer—which, I guess would not be much different than how most of us will die, anyway. But you shouldn't rush these things."

:: Topic 17 :: Forks, spoons, and knives...yay plastic wear!

George eyed a box of plastic wear. "I bet I could eat those."

"Now see here, those are for the picnic."

"Oh yeah. We're late for the picnic!"

:: Topic 18 :: Bristle blocks!!!!!!!!

"Quite right! How could I have forgotten! Quick, grab the Bristle Blocks for little Timmy!"

"And the music, don't forget the music!"

:: Topic 19 :: Journey to polycarbonate

"Journey it is."

"Not that crap! Pick out something better. I'll get the polycarbonate picnic windows!"

"Hmm. Why are we taking polycarbonate windows?"

"Because it's the only way we could work polycarbonate into the story!"

"Oh yeah. We had to go from Journey to polycarbonate, somehow."

:: Topic 20 :: Broken CD of terror

Fred looked through the CD rack. His fingers paused on one labeled: *Nonstop Journey Hits*. He pulled it out and looked at a post-it note on the outside of the plastic case. The post-it read: "Broken CD of Terror! Only plays the first song, then skips back to the beginning!"

"Perfect," Fred said.

:: Topic 21 :: Attack of my favorite Martian

George and Fred nearly had everything in the car before a Martian appeared before them!

"What's up?" said the Martian.

George wondered that himself, but Fred told him, "It's cool, George. It's my favorite Martian, XvYpRtLq! He likes to attack people, but only with dull stories."

"Oh. Cool," George said dishonestly.

:: Topic 22 :: Knowing that the center of the solar eclipse ate my sister's car, and how I slept through it

"Greetings, Earthlings! I just got back from the center of the solar eclipse that ate my sister's car."

"A solar eclipse! How was it?" Fred asked.

"I don't know. I slept through it. It had been a long night previously; I was hanging out where time was slowing down and everything."

:: Topic 23 :: Only in my dream can I fly (except on Pluto)

George said, "You are not making any sense at all, Martian, but...can you fly? Because that would be cool."

"In my dreams I can fly! Except on Pluto."

"You mean there's something weird about when you dream on Pluto?"

"No, I just never sleep on Pluto—it's a total party planet—so I never dream there."

"So, what brings you to Earth, today?" Fred asked.

:: Topic 24 :: The Blob is coming! The holiest of blobs, and careful swamp monsters!

"If you don't mind my telling you, I am here to announce that the Blob is coming!"

"That great big monster from the movies?!" George asked.

"No, the reincarnation of the Buddha. Humans, he has gained some weight, let me tell you. And look out, swamp monsters, because he is HUNGRY!"

"Shit. So am I," said George. "We gotta' get to this picnic."

:: Topic 25 :: The dragon's lair

"I'm sorry, George," said the Martian. "You will never get to eat."

"Why?"

"Because you don't have time. There is only one topic left and once it is said—"

"Don't say it!" George screamed.

"Once it is said, the story will be over."

"Quick, to the picnic! I need food!"

Fred and George hopped in the car, sped to the picnic, met their friends there, and ran to the grill, where there was a stack of burgers on a plate.

"Too hot!" George said, trying to pick one up. "I need buns!"

"You need what?" Alice asked. She walked toward them, her hips waving from side to side like the ocean's tide. Or something.

"Uh...I need...buns?"

"Oh baby, you always did flirt well. Remember our first time hanging out together?"

"No. Shut up!"

"We met at Video Palace Harbor Kingdom Mania and stayed until closing, playing that one game, over and over."

"That was a long time ago. And besides, they are open 24 hours."

"Not on Christmas! But don't tell me you don't remember—the name of the game became our mating cry!"

"Who are you again?" George said.

"I still can't make love without crying out, DRAGON'S LAIR! DRAGON'S LAIR!!!!"

1 This line was a link that went to a "news of the weird" type Web page stating this as fact.

2 "This Week in Cake" was an excellent feature by a blogger who has since discontinued the series. This link went to a particularly tasty looking green tea cake.

3 This link went to a newspaper article discussing the phenomenon.

I don't usually like to do reviews of contemporary
stuff—there are always people covering that area
already and a lot of them do it well. But I love
picking on a classic and pointing out the absurdity
that should be readily apparent in it (yet, no one
really cared when this game came out that it had
nothing to do with any sort of realistic jousting).

It's a highly entertaining game, though.
One of my favorites.

And Now It's Time To Review A Classic: Joust

Joust. What a lovely game.

And oh, the realism! Granted, most jousts were between only *two* people on flying ostriches, not a whole bunch of them. Also, jousts didn't usually take place in a multi-tiered cavern with lava monsters but the game did get the basic principle right: be higher than your opponent.

Yes, the knights of old had only to be sure they rode the flying ostrich capable of achieving the greater height—otherwise, they would vanish into thin air when their opponent's lance touched them. Nobody wanted that!

I love Camus' ability to write about little things. Hanging out on balconies or smoking cigarettes or when he is describing someone's apartment—he approaches all these details with grace and simplicity.

This is more a parody of *The Stranger* than of Camus' body of work, so if you haven't read that book (perhaps his finest), you may not get all of the jokes.

There was an element of sexism in this piece that made me apprehensive about posting it. By parodying such a limited portion of Camus' novel, you may not be aware that this was just one character's perspective among various characters in a full novel and that the narrator is agreeing with him because of the narrator's apathy, not because of a shared point of view. I didn't want to include this piece in the book without at least pointing that out. It is wrong to smack people around.

Oh yeah—and I really did have an Atari die on me, which inspired this blog at least in part. I had this Atari Lynx (they made the sweetest games for that thing) and I broke it out one night, intending to stay up late playing every game I had for it, but it just wouldn't work. I never figured out what was wrong with it, but I tried everything. Eventually, I really did just dump it in the trash.

November 23, 2005

Oh Camus, you are appreciated, still

My Atari died today. Or maybe it was yesterday, I can't tell. I haven't used it in a while so it's possible that it died last year or perhaps the year before that.

After putting the Atari in the garbage, I wandered about the apartment. I opened a window and looked at the tree out front. Its leaves were orange. The sky was hazy and the street was wet. Several cars had their lights on. A woman passed by in a red coat. Two bums stumbled up the street, arguing loudly. A couple walked slowly around the corner and entered the pastry shop.

I moved the ashtray from the window to the coffee table and smoked a cigarette while opening mail. There was a bill from the water company. There were photos of my niece. I recycled a postcard advertisement from Comcast.

I smoked another cigarette while standing in the middle of the room. I didn't feel like doing anything.

There was a knock at the door and I answered. Drummond asked, "I have some fake sausage and whiskey. How about dinner at my place?" I accepted, as it would save me the trouble of cooking.

His apartment smelled of old books. "I offered dinner because I have a favor to ask of you," he said. I drank the whiskey. He proceeded to explain that he had been playing his Xbox until just last week. "It started treating me poorly, so I quit playing. But then I felt guilty, so I went back to the last game I saved and tried to get to level twelve. Well, little do I know, the Xbox must think its job is to frustrate me because it won't let me even get close to level twelve. It's just not having it, no matter how hard I try."

I lit a cigarette and watched him pour more whiskey. He told me that he broke up with the Xbox, would never play it again and that he even smacked it around a little. He said he had never smacked it around before, but he thought that, just this once, it was justified.

Drummond looked upset. He leaned over the table to ask me, "So, since you're a man, I want to know. Did I handle the situation correctly?"

I nodded. He seemed pleased.

I wrote this after a plane ride to Iowa, during
which I had time to read most of Dave Eggers'
A Heartbreaking Work of Staggering Genius.
Later, I was shopping for Thanksgiving with the
family and bits of this blog started popping into
my head. Since I had just read Eggers, they were
coming out in his sort of repetitive, mantra-like
style. So I went with it.

      Naturally, there is no way any of this is
as good as the original writer's material. It isn't
meant to be. It was fun writing it, though.

      In case you haven't read that book yet,
I'm going to give you the quick review: it is what it
says it is. It's a genius tale of heartbreak. But I'll
also give you this disclaimer: it took me 96 pages
to start liking it, because it took me that long to
figure out what he was doing.

Oh Eggers, may you be appreciated ever more

We are Thanksgiving grocery shoppers. We are the best. *We are taking care of it all*. We are Thanksgiving grocery shoppers.

Mom wants eight good tomatoes. She holds up her finger and thumb, saying, "Just this size." But she doesn't need to say that because I know. I know everything. *I just know*. That's how good I am, how good we all are. We just know.

I am getting pears when my sister calls. She's in the store. She's a Thanksgiving grocery shopper. She is the best. She knows, because she is the best, you see—She knows that I am near the cucumbers.

"How many?" I ask.

"Two."

"Is that it?"

"Yep."

And that's all. That's all we need to say. The seven pies that must be made, the twenty pounds of potatoes to be mashed, the crowded grocery store—None of it will get to us. We know how to deal with it. We use two carts and cell phones and we enjoy it and *we take care of it all*. We are the best. We are Thanksgiving grocery shoppers.

Ernest Hemingway opened up a lot of writers, myself included, to the possibility that saying less is often far more. If you are writing about a train trip, for example, and the train goes by an old church, then you can just write, "an old church." Let the reader's mind fill in the details and get on with the story.

This is significant in so many ways, but one of them is that the reader does not have to become estranged by description that doesn't match their experience. Most people can imagine an old church. Sometimes, it's not important to the story what the church looks like, so why describe it?

Another thing that Hemingway did was challenge masculinity. He had some macho characters, sure, and they typically did macho things (they would follow sports or go hunting a lot or they would be boxers, for example). But he challenged masculinity by giving his male characters particular weaknesses. *The Sun Also Rises* is possibly his best work and it features an impotent male protagonist.

Unfortunately, his male characters are often saved from having to go through the challenge of commitment to a relationship. This piece in particular examines the rather convenient death at the end of *A Farewell to Arms.* So I parodied that a little and his use of the seasons and of course, I couldn't help but pick on him for his long extended dialogs in which the reader can easily lose track of who is speaking.

Oh Hemingway, you will be appreciated ever more

It was a good fall. The air was dry and crisp. The trees had chosen a shade of orange unequalled by previous years. It was the sort of fall that would allow armies to win battles and soldiers to fall in love with nurses.

In a small hovelled bar atop the hill an old man sat. He sipped his coffee. He was dressed as a fisherman. He hadn't been to sea in over seven seasons.

He motioned to the barkeep, who responded by refilling his mug.

Through the door came an Englishman. He was spry, though his face shown an age similar to the fisherman's. He stumbled to the bar. Recognizing the old man next to him, he shouted, "Ahoy there, silly old codger. I'm a little tight already, but why not have another, eh?"

"Why not, indeed, Sir Stefan?"

"What brings a good sir like you to the bar in the afternoon? Ah, yes, Rudolfo is always here, isn't he? I had forgotten."

Stefan chuckled. He scraped his knuckles against Rudolfo's ribs good-naturedly. "No, seriously, I hadn't forgotten."

"Why don't you tell me the news of the baseball?"

"I will, with pleasure. Canseco has surprised the world by entering the Japanese league at the age of sixty-two!"

"Sixty-two? He can't hope to compete at that age."

"Well, they say his legs have been replaced with robot legs."

"Ah, yes, well then...."

"I think I'm going to have the same thing done to mine."

"A good idea."

"I think so."

"And just to be polite, I'm afraid I must ask for news about the wife?"

"Ah, she's just about dead now after hanging on for eight rough months."

"I see. And the mistress?"

"I'm afraid she's in the same condition."

"I see."

"Yes."

"Barkeep! We'll both have another of what he's got. On his tab."

"Coming up," said the barkeep.

"So, it's just a matter of time, then, eh?"

"What is?"

"We'll be dead in our tracks. The old death monster will have caught us."

"Quite true. Quite true. You first, though, I imagine."

"Why do you say that?"

"Well, you're the older one, aren't you?"

"I don't know. I've forgotten who was talking."

"Yes, a bit of a drag, isn't it—these long, strung out dialogs?"

"Certainly."

"Well, surely we can figure out which of us is which."

"I agree. I believe I'm the one with the sense of humor."

"I was going to say I was, but perhaps that's just wishful thinking."

The old men looked to the window, drawn by the sound of water tapping lightly on wood.

"It's started to rain."

"Oh my."

But by the time the man had said, "Oh my," the other was lying on the floor of the bar looking quite dead.

"Oh my."

The barkeep refilled his drink.

I created this image one day, using a photo I took
in New Mexico. I added a falling person, because
I thought that would be funny somehow. Then I
decided that it would be even funnier if I added
arrows to describe how the person bounced off the
roof and landed on the ground.

It was a simple extension of logic that led
me to transcribe a fictional court case regarding
the incident.

The People
vs.
The Church That I Once Took A Picture Of

I have gathered the following excerpts from the courtroom proceedings.

Reprinted with permission.

THE JUDGE: Order in the court! Order in the court!

[SOUND OF MALLET POUNDING]

THE PROSECUTION: Please state your name and occupation for the record.

BOB FILLMORE: My name is Bob Fillmore. I'm a retired historian, with a specialty in the history of the church.

THE PROSECUTION: And you also happened to see Larry the Comedian fall from the sky and be killed by the church?

THE DEFENSE: Objection, Your Honor. That's for the jury to decide.

THE JUDGE: Sustained. The prosecution may, however, rephrase their question if they do not wish to test my patience.

THE PROSECUTION: Mr. Fillmore, did you or did you not see Larry the Comedian fall from the sky and impact with the church?

BOB FILLMORE: Well, yes, although he did bounce off and wind up on the ground.

THE PROSECUTION: Did you see the church move to try to avoid this fatal contact?

BOB FILLMORE: No, sir. I did not.

THE PROSECUTION: Very well. I would like to ask you if you're familiar with the history of the construction of the church?

BOB FILLMORE: Very familiar. Most likely, I can tell you anything you would like to know.

THE PROSECUTION: Mr. Fillmore, I'd like to know if there were plans for the church before the church was built.

BOB FILLMORE: Well, yes, there were, certainly. You don't just go building a church wherever. You have to figure out exactly where you're going to build it.

THE PROSECUTION: That's right. And the church had been put right on the spot that Larry the Comedian happened to be falling toward on the fateful day in question.

BOB FILLMORE: Yes, apparently so.

THE PROSECUTION: And, just to clear something up. The church—it doesn't often take walks or go on vacations, correct?

THE DEFENSE: Objection, Your Honor. He's leading the witness.

THE JUDGE: Overruled. I would like to know the answer to the question.

BOB FILLMORE: Well, no, the church as far as I know has never moved from that spot. Once it was decided where she was to be built, that's where she stayed.

THE PROSECUTION: Indeed. Ladies and gentlemen of the jury, Mr. Fillmore's testimony clearly shows proof of premeditation!

THE DEFENSE: Objection!

[POUNDING OF MALLET]

THE JUDGE: Sustained. Prosecution should save leaps of judgment for the closing arguments.

———————

SHELLY MCPHERSON: My name is Shelly McPherson. I was the coroner on duty during the day in question. I also serve as forensics expert for Sheriff Walt.

THE PROSECUTION: Let's get straight to the point. Was Larry the Comedian dead when you found him?

SHELLY MCPHERSON: Yes.

THE PROSECUTION: What, in your opinion, had killed Larry the Comedian?

SHELLY MCPHERSON: I determined that the most likely cause of death was the second impact to his body, done by the tower of the church.

THE PROSECUTION: Not the subsequent landing on the sidewalk?

SHELLY MCPHERSON: No. In my professional opinion, Larry the Comedian was dead by the time he was struck by the sidewalk. He impacted with the roof of the main hall of the church, then bounced off and was killed when he hit the tower, which he then bounced off and landed on the sidewalk. I have diagrammed it here.

Diagram by Sally McPherson, rendered in pastels, then photocopied for the court

---

THE JUDGE: Closing argument for the prosecution.

THE PROSECUTION: Had Larry the Comedian not been struck by the murderous church, he may very well have been sitting in the courtroom with us today.

[SOBS AND MOANS]

THE PROSECUTION: Testimony has shown that the church premeditated its location for the purpose of striking fatal blows against Larry far in the future. We have presented you all the evidence you need to convict the church of 1st degree murder—the murder of...Larry the Comedian. It is your duty to put this evil church behind bars, so that this heinous act cannot be repeated and people can once more feel free to fall from the sky whenever and wherever they choose.

Growing up, my sisters would force me to judge
Barbie doll beauty pageants that lasted for hours.
And by "force" I mean that no one would play with
me otherwise.

However, I did enjoy trying to think up
questions for the interview round. Unlike the
questions in this blog, I wrote questions that were
funny and entertaining, so at least I got to focus
my energy creatively during my youth.

I am a judge in a Barbie doll fashion contest!

And it's time for the judge's questions!

JUDGE: Contessa, my, aren't you a manly-looking woman. You must work out, or something. Tell me how it is that you developed this masculine physique you've got going.

CONTESSA: Um, we only have three female Barbie dolls so ask another question.

JUDGE: All right, but you'll be docked some points for that response. So, how do you think you could help the world by winning this pageant?

CONTESSA: I'm very proud of my skills as a typist. So, if I win the prize money, I'll use it to support myself while I offer my typing skills to charity.

JUDGE: Very good. And now for Irene's question. Irene, where did you say you were from?

IRENE: Nantuckettoma, Can-tuck-ee!

JUDGE: Very good. And now for Candace's question—

IRENE: That was my question?

JUDGE: Irene, you did very well so don't make me dock you.

IRENE: I'm sorry.

JUDGE: And now, Candace—

DARLA: I'm Darla. Darla from Rhode Island. Candace goes last.

JUDGE: Oh yes, my apologies. You all have the exact same plastic face and body so it's hard for me to tell you apart (not counting Contessa, of course).

DARLA: I tend to wear more spring colors.

JUDGE: Uh...yeah.......... Thanks, that helps a lot.... Really. Anyway, what would you say is your finest attribute?

DARLA: Well, all the other females in my world have the exact same body as me, so I would have to say it's my brain.

JUDGE: So, you're very intelligent.

DARLA: Well, that too, but my brain is very beautiful. I was told that once by a professional phrenologist.

JUDGE: Ah. Okay then, good answer. And now, Candace—

CANDACE: Yes?

JUDGE: You're not really wearing any clothes, are you?

CANDACE: After seven evening gowns, three swimwear and sixteen casual, we ran out of clothes so shut up.

JUDGE: All right. Um....

CANDACE: Was that my question?

JUDGE: No. Uh, do you have any pets?

CANDACE: I have two turtles named Binky and Froggy.

JUDGE: And would you eat them for dinner if someone gave you one hundred dollars to do it?

CANDACE: Uh. No?

JUDGE: Very good. All right then, it's time for the tally of scores.

[TWENTY MINUTE PAUSE]

JUDGE: In third place, with 4,236 points, it's Darla! Yay! And in second place with 4,238 points, it's Irene from Can—tuck—ee! Yay! Way to go, Irene! And now, the announcement you've all been waiting for—the winner of the beauty pageant after all these hours of fun!

CANDACE: Just say it, Aaron.

JUDGE: The winner is...Contessa with 4,239 points! Nice job, Contessa! Candace came in fourth with 4,235 points. Now will you play LEGOs with me?

IRENE: All right. But only for ten minutes, as we agreed.

Rhode Island:
A Public Relations Gimmick Gone Too Far?

There are some roads, sure,
    and maybe even a few Rhodes scholars,
        but it sure as hell isn't an island.

I didn't want to capitalize the word "cancer," so I very purposely used lower case for this title.

It's true that more and more people, percentage-wise, are surviving the experience, but it's also true that more and more people are getting it.

This was as positive as I was able to be about the subject.

The good thing about cancer

I have a good friend who has been told she has months to live. You never know about these things, for sure, but that's what she's been told.

Her husband is also a good friend and we've been in communication. I call often, though it is rare that we connect. The few times we've talked were hasty exchanges, basic updates of the situation—it's not easy to do these things over the phone and we are 1332.7 miles apart.

The last time we spoke, we each said, "I love you." That's difficult for two heterosexual males to do without it being some kind of struggle. But it wasn't. Not now. The impact of the situation has raised our awareness beyond the need to worry about ridiculous social constraints.

If one case of cancer can do that to two people—raise their awareness to that extent—then the world should become increasingly more aware as more people get cancer. In fact, I feel it is inevitable.

We do need to find positive things amid disaster,
even if it only makes us laugh for a second. When
disaster is all you've got, make disaster-ade!

My 9-11 experience wasn't that
remarkable. I had been having recurring
dreams during the week preceding—not dreams
of disaster necessarily, but horrible dreams of
nightmarish martial law, filled with people that
were afraid and hiding all the time. When I woke
up on September 11, I just didn't feel good. I
couldn't figure out why—I felt healthy, just...
wrong somehow. I decided I'd call in sick that
day.

A friend phoned just after the first plane
hit. We were on the phone together when the next
plane hit and we were still on the phone after the
towers were rubble.

That day, I coped by making a mixed
CD for a friend. I left the TV on for a while,
but eventually I had to shut it off, shut out the
repeated images.

After dark I went for a walk. I wound up
at the independent movie rental shop and walked
around in there for about an hour. There was
nothing I wanted to see.

Walking back, I saw people on their
front steps, talking on cell phones. I saw people
wandering around, like I was doing. I hadn't seen
this many people outside their homes in...well,
forever.

When I ask myself, "how does this hurt
me?" the response is muddled.

The Good Thing About
When People Fly Planes Into Buildings

In September of 2001, I had recently ended a ten-month relationship that had been a rebound from a six-year relationship. In short, I was truly single for the first time in about seven years.

I started doing a lot of writing in coffee shops and for some strange reason, all kinds of young, attractive women began to initiate conversations with me. Never having experienced such success with females, I thought, "At last, the world has recognized me as its foremost attractive male specimen! They can sense my virility and the fact that I am single! Huzzah!"

However, as months drifted by, I soon realized that my newly discovered virility was no longer working. Here I was, being selective, as it was clear that all women wanted me, and suddenly no woman would come near me. Naturally, I was baffled.

Hindsight allowed me to connect events and I realized that it wasn't any sort of waxing and waning of my virility—it was simply that September of 2001 was such a lonely and desperate time for people that many women stooped far below their ordinary standards to talk to me. For that, I thank them.

Here's the deal: I'm not saying that I'll jump for joy at the next American catastrophe, but if it happens, be sure that I will be out there respectfully spanking as many asses of lonely and desperate women as I can get my hands on.

After all, it is our patriotic duty to make the most of foul times.

I never really wanted to do a blog on George Bush—
he's too easy of a target. But a reader of mine that
went by Stupidhead won a contest and her prize
was that she got to choose a blog topic of mine. She
chose George Bush.

To some people, this wasn't clear: I was
poking fun at the President's reaction during the
September 11 disaster by turning his uninterrupted
appearance at a school into his first "meeting."

A Transcript: President Bush's First Meeting
On September 11, 2001

PRESIDENT GEORGE BUSH: I'm sure we've all got questions. I've got questions. Let's start with some questions. Anyone want to start?

SALLY MATHESON: Why don't you start, Mr. President?

BUSH: Okay. Well, the first thing that comes to my mind is, how come the caterpillar was so hungry? That darned caterpillar ate up all that stuff. How'd he get so hungry?

BILLY JORGENSEN: My big brother says that when he smokes pot he gets all starving.

BUSH: Yeah, I've uh...I've heard that. Not like cocaine, is it?

JORGENSEN: What's coke-ane?

BUSH: It's uh...it's a special kinda' coke.

MILLIE PETERS: Do you like it?

BUSH: I've uh...I actually don't know what you're talkin' about.

PETERS: About the coke-ane, silly!

BUSH: Yeah, uh...so any more questions about the book? I'd love to talkinate with you all about this here litera—...liter...this here book.

JIMMY DOBBINS: Why are your nose hairs gray?

BUSH: Well, that's a...that's a condition. Er, not a condition except in that it's a condition of bein'. Like bein' a condition. Of age. It's an age thing, you see, when a duck gets old, the gander...uh...when a duck gets old he takes a gander at a goose.

DOBBINS: Is that why hairs grow out of grown-ups' moles?

[SILENCE]

BUSH: Andrew?

CHIEF OF STAFF ANDREW CARD: [UNINTELLIGIBLE WHISPERS]

BUSH: Uh...yes.

RACHEL SMITH: Why do you think the caterpillar was so hungry?

BUSH: Well, I uh...I think he was just concerned, you know. He was thinkin' of all those other countries out there that might get his food and well...he just...well see, if you count all your chickens and they're hatched, well then shame on you. And if uh...if you count all your chickens and they try to bite you, well then, uh...I can count, if that's what you're asking. If you're asking me, as the president, if I can count, well yes, ma'am, I'll tell you in three words that I can count good.

If you don't know your history...

...you are doomed to repeat it.

But that's okay, because you'll never know you're repeating it, since you don't know it in the first place.

So it's all good.

If a tsunami takes out entire islands, the United
States media has an estimate of how many died
within minutes. Hurricane Katrina hit and days
went by without a widely known death toll. In
fact, I'm still not sure what the total was.
        United States citizens were appalled
when it was discovered that the U.S.S.R. withheld
information about the disaster at the Chernobyl
nuclear power plant. Is there a parallel here?

Where is your
magic death toll counting machine now?

Do we only use it when the catastrophe can be blamed on terrorists?

Or when the catastrophe is happening in another country?

Or, perhaps we only use it when we have NOT been an enabler of those deaths due to our own gross negligence in overseeing the crisis?

Tell us how bad it is so we can rub your nose in it, politicos.

I tend to stay away from groups and group activism.
I mean, I'll sign petitions and I get a lot of action
alerts by email, but in general, I just prefer to work
alone. That doesn't mean that there aren't any
socially conscious activities that I can perform. In
fact, there are a lot of things that just one person
can do and I believe they go a long way toward
making a difference. This blog is kind of about
this. While I recognize the importance of banding
together to fight a common foe, I tend to focus my
energy on much smaller problems.

I do have the phrase "Defender of Obscure
Social Interests" on various online profiles.
However, there was no Jacques Dominique that
sent me this letter. I wrote it, used a few automatic
language translators to create the pseudo-bad
English, and added my response. What was
challenging in this piece was that I wanted to pick a
real cause, yet I wanted to turn the person down, so
whatever the person was asking me to do had to be
harmless enough that I didn't look too insensitive
in my refusal to act—otherwise, it would have been
harder to laugh.

DECEMBER 8, 2005

A Fan Letter from Jacques Dominique

Dear Aaron Dietz,

I am a reader of a lot of time of its blogs and the joy. But today I write to ask a favor.

In you profile, says that you are a "Defender of Obscure Social Interests." Well, I am a member of the Group of Support of Haiti, an association of individuals that maintain the Haitian people in his fight for the justice, for the human rights, and for the participatory democracy. Although there is now a formal democracy in Haiti, the poor majority he continues to be excluded of the process.

By subscribing to our bulletin, you will be capable of helping us unite with organizations of the local level there and still more the cause of the justice for a people that are needed. I thanks for its aid.

Sincerely,

Jacques Dominique

Dear Jacques,

I would love to help you but your cause is just not obscure enough. I really do have a deep level of commitment to fighting for obscure social interests, but the cause has to be a lot more obscure than the one you have written me about.

As you may have noticed, there are actually quite a few poor people in Haiti and this makes their situation not so much obscure as disastrous and incredibly harrowing. So, you see, it is just not my thing.

Examples of obscure social interests I have taken up in the past are these:

1. Will LEGO release a Black LEGO figurine? (They now have.)

2. Will libraries adopt a best practice book for labeling materials? (this, I'm still working on.)

I wish you luck, and if your cause happens to grow much more obscure in the future (like, say, if you get the number of poor people down to about two or three), please feel free to approach me again.

aaron

I think just about everything in this blog is true,
to my recollection (though I've changed one
name). I was in contact with LEGO and I truly
was frustrated that they didn't have a Black LEGO
figurine. They did release the basketball players
shortly after I started bugging them and Lando
soon after that, which was a sigh of relief. I have
five Rubbermaid tubs filled with LEGO bricks, so I
didn't want to accept that all of those LEGO bricks
were produced by a racist company.

All in all, if this weren't true, it wouldn't
even be blog-worthy, since it takes way too long
to get to a subpar punch line. Since it's true, it's
mildly interesting.

And here is just one reason why
I am better than you

Why am I better than you?

It's because I care.

As evidence of my caring, I'm going to tell you a true story:

When LEGO started coming out with Star Wars LEGO sets, I was incredibly pleased. I started collecting as many as I could afford, but in time, I noticed a glaring problem in their new product line: Lobot, a white, male assistant to Lando Calrissian was released as a LEGO figure, while at the time there were still no figures for Lando Calrissian (who happens to be Black and run an entire city and mining operation) or Mace Windu (also a Black character from the Star Wars universe).

How can you release a white male assistant with nary a line in one of the movies before you release his boss: the man that led the attack on the second Death Star?!

Obviously I feared it was because he was Black. I looked around at all my LEGO figures...all yellow faces. I thought about what I knew about the company's origins—a Nordic CEO, the grandson of the creator of the company.... Could LEGO be racist?!

So I did what every good citizen of the United States would do. I complained. I emailed LEGO and got a response from "Maggie," a very polite and capable customer service representative. She told me that the company chose yellow as a universal color, so that each child could decide what nationality that child's LEGO figures were.

I was like, "Hey, that's cool. Just release a yellow-faced Lando, then."

Over the course of several weeks, there were emails back and forth, and a few months later, guess what was released as a seemingly last-minute addition to LEGO's basketball series? Black men. Yes, and even a Chinese man, if I remember right.

They released sets based on real live NBA players out of the blue. They didn't come with any of the basketball sets—those were already released and in stores, but you could suddenly buy "real" minority LEGO figures in packs of three—

nothing else in the set, just the three guys that started the march toward equality for the LEGO company.

And guess who was introduced during the next big Star Wars product release (and who happened to have possibly the biggest picture of a LEGO figure ever to grace the inside of a LEGO catalog): Lando Calrissian, standing in front of his LEGO Cloud City. He was so prominent on the page that he probably used up more ink than the entire city. They apparently really wanted you to notice something, eh?

So, that is my evidence. Now you cannot doubt that I care. Do you care? I didn't think so. And that is why I am better than you.

I can't tell you how much I love white
tea. I'm drinking some right now and
it is heavenly.

And now,
another reason why I am better than you

I drink white tea. That's right. You've heard of the fantastic effects that green tea can have on a person: healthy heart, long life, hallucinations, etc. Well, white tea is even better.

I will now tell you why so that you can't look it up on the Internet and claim to have already known.

White tea is the same thing as green tea. That's why it's so much better.

Got it?

Okay, you still need some explanation? Well, all right, since I'm so much better than you I will explain further: white tea is green tea buds picked at their finest moment. How fine is that moment? They can only pick white tea buds two days out of the entire year, that's how fine. White tea is so precious that it once was reserved for emperors and nobility!

But now, I drink it.

Once, The Redhead offered to buy me lunch at a
place down the street, but I was drinking white
tea. If I had gone with her, the tea would have
been wasted. The free lunch would have been
equal to many bags of white tea, so, financially,
it would have been worth the free lunch to waste
the tea. But I love white tea so much that I try to
honor it. It would be foul to make a cup of white
tea and only drink half. I turned down the free
lunch and finished the tea sitting on the front
steps of my apartment building. It was a lovely
time.

And here is yet another reason why
I am better than you

It's not just because I drink white tea. All of the long-time readers have caught on to that (I bet you're all doing it, now). No, I am better than you because I give white tea the respect it deserves.

For example, I don't eat or drink anything else while I am drinking white tea.

I always use each bag of white tea twice, because it would be a shame to waste a precious bit of white tea that still had flavor in it.

I even brush my teeth and rinse my palate with water before drinking it, so that I'll be able to appreciate the full splendor of white tea uncontaminated by other tastes.

Also, when people tell me white tea sucks, I put out a contract on their life.

And that is why I am better than you.

This is an alternate version of the previous blog. I
liked them both, but they didn't really go together,
so I posted them on different blog sites. I decided
to include them both because I still can't choose
between them....

OCTOBER 24, 2005

And here is yet another reason why
I am better than you

It's not just because I drink white tea. I covered that long ago. It's old news. In fact, you are all probably drinking white tea in an attempt to be as awesome as I am. But I ask you, do you do it like this?!

Tea minus 3 hr 00 min :: Begin two hour meditation to prepare the spirit
Tea minus 1 hr 00 min :: Remove self from reality to avoid distractions
Tea minus 0 hr 45 min :: Cleanse the body by scrubbing with metal brush
Tea minus 0 hr 15 min :: Brush the teeth and tongue and upper palate
Tea minus 0 hr 10 min :: Insert tea kettle in high-radiation "purifying" device
Tea minus 0 hr 05 min :: Begin heating water blessed by Tibetan monks
Tea minus 0 hr 03 min :: Get naked
Tea minus 0 hr 02 min :: Prepare brand new mug, taken out of plastic wrap
Tea minus 0 hr 01 min :: Place one bag white tea in mug using sterile tweezers
Tea minus 0 hr 00 min :: Pour water in mug

Enjoy (after letting it steep, you dufus)!

In addition to white tea, I am also obsessed with Everest gum. It has artificial sweetener in it, like most gums, but I can't help chewing it. I like to have fresh breath and this gum—when you put it in your mouth for the first time, it clears your sinuses with the peppermint scent.

Plus, Everest gum comes in smaller pieces than most gums. I don't need a whole big slice of gum, especially since you don't want to look like you're chewing tobacco or something (especially at a business meeting). So the size is right, too.

In any case, ever since I became such a fan of it, I've noticed that supply sources for this gum have been dwindling. I can't say for sure if this is because of some conspiratorial plot against me, but it is true that I have had to go to great lengths to track this gum down.

JANUARY 5, 2006

I have beaten you, CIA Agent Jones!

Or Johnson or whatever your name is.

I admit. It was kind of funny when you got assigned to me and had nothing better to do than eliminate all sources of my favorite gum, Everest.

And it took me a while to figure out what had happened, too. I was living in Denver at the time and even contacted the company. When they responded, listing several places that I knew *used to* carry Everest, I realized something was up. Obviously, you were intercepting the shipments that were supposed to go to Target and 7-Eleven. And everywhere else in Denver, too.

But then I found that little convenience store inside the new Webb Building. You didn't think about that place, did you?! Or maybe you thought it was hilarious to watch me go through security just to buy a tin of Everest gum.

Ha. Real funny, Agent Jones. I got wise to you in the end, though—I bought online. Yes, you made sure Everest's direct purchase Web form was not working but you couldn't stop candydirect.com, could you? Of course, I had to buy a case, but if you refrigerate them they stay pretty fresh.

Now I've moved to Seattle. At first, I saw Everest everywhere. I thought, "Did Agent Jones get reassigned? Did he not want to relocate?"

I soon realized—you knew I still had half of that case of Everest left. So you were biding your time, making me feel secure about my ability to buy Everest in all of the places that Everest's customer service representative told me I should be able to buy it.

But as soon as the case of Everest was down to its last tin of gum I realized: Everest was nowhere. I checked Target, 7-Eleven and all those other corporate chains and could not find it!

You are a wily one, you!

But you see, I found a source. I found a place in Seattle where I can buy Everest and I don't even have to go through a metal detector! And I'm not telling you where it is, Agent Jones!

This blog was not entirely true. I had found a
source for Everest—that was true enough—but
it wasn't tainted. Agent Jones didn't switch the
Peppermint flavor for the Wintergreen (an entirely
inadequate flavor by comparison). However, I
did pull an Everest tin out of the refrigerator and
look at it in strange lighting—for just a second,
I thought it said Wintergreen. That was the
moment that inspired this blog.

So you see, I'm not opposed to making
stuff up if it's entertaining.

CIA Agent Jones Tricked Me!

I should not have underestimated him.

Remember how I found a source for my Everest gum, despite an evil CIA plot to make my life miserable?

Well, I broke open a tin from the new source and what do you know? It is not the Peppermint kind. It is the Wintergreen flavor. Agent Jones tricked me!

I wasted no time in buying out my source of Everest gum and apparently I was so excited at finding it that I didn't see it was the wrong flavor! I mean, Wintergreen is okay, but only the Peppermint freshens my breath well enough.

I'll get you for this, Agent Jones!

This one isn't so funny, but I left it in to complete
the Everest Conspiracy trilogy.
 It's probably for the better that he won,
since aspartame is most likely very bad for
humans.

You Win, CIA Agent Jones

Do you remember when CIA Agent Jones made my life miserable by forcing me to go to extreme measures just to get my favorite breath-freshening, potentially cancer-causing chewing gum?

Do you remember when I finally found a source in Seattle where I could buy Everest, only to find that Agent Jones had tricked me into buying the wrong flavor?

Well, I found yet another source and I went there the other day to buy more, only to find that Agent Jones had finally won the game. There was a big empty space where the Everest should have been. I asked a sales person if they would be getting more in and he laughed in my face. Then, he remembered how impolite that was and got serious again.

"I don't think so," he said, hoping I would go away quickly so that he could laugh at me as he told his co-workers.

You see, I'm afraid Agent Jones has gone and shut down the whole company, just to keep me from buying my favorite gum. I can't even get it from candydirect.com anymore, and Everest's official Web site (everestgum.com), is now unavailable.

I give up, Agent Jones. You win.

It does get tiresome to have all of your favorite
products disappear just because you like them.
    I like this blog because it's about
coincidences arranging circumstances. If I hadn't
run out of deoderant none of this would have
happened. Though, I suppose one could argue
that not much, really, happened anyway, but oh
well.

How My Allergy Caused Me To Harass A Woman

Random calamitous events led me to harass my poor, attractive, female neighbor.

It started with my deodorant: I ran out.

I couldn't find the Burt's Bees deodorant I use anywhere in my neighborhood (this is a conspiracy I'm quite familiar with, so it was no surprise). So I bought a different kind: organic, seemed to have a nice aroma. And lo and behold, a rash broke out under my armpits each time I used it.

No problem, right? I promptly ordered some Burt's Bees deodorant online

However, apparently in order to receive a package of deodorant from Burt's Bees, a signature is required. Again, no problem. I'm unemployed. At home most of the day. Piece of cake.

Well, it's not a piece of cake. I don't own a landline phone because I threw mine in a ditch, so no one can buzz my apartment. Thus, I received a "1st Attempt" delivery notice from UPS.

Now, the next morning, I concocted a fantastic plan: I would buy a phone. And asparagus. So I bought a phone. And asparagus.

On my way back from my errands, I saw a UPS truck! I could see the "2nd Attempt" notice on my door down the block, so I decided to hang out with my groceries and wait for the UPS driver to return to his truck.

While I waited, an attractive woman passed by. Even though nothing of note occurred during the passing-by, this is key to the story.

When the UPS driver returned, he explained that, unfortunately, my notice was left by another driver. Apparently, I live near the line that divides routes. Quite interesting, no? No.

Anyway, when I got back to my apartment, someone down the hall opened their door. In an amazing demonstration of why you shouldn't bitch-slap strangers because they might happen to find out where you live some day, the attractive woman I saw earlier came out the door!

Naturally, I assumed there was some sort of bond between us because obviously any stranger you see more than once and are attracted to, you are bound to engage in intercourse with, even if they didn't notice you at all. There's no need to explain the logic behind *that* conclusion.

So, I said, "Hey," and asked her how she was. Pretty bold, I know.

Incidentally, while writing this blog, I saw my UPS truck pull up to my building. I have since intercepted my Burt's Bees deodorant and can now smell nice once again.

Zorgnarf: Alien Inventor

This really baffled me. What do you do when you
find underwear right outside someone's door?
I stood there, for a minute, trying to figure out
whether to knock, knock-and-run, or just do
nothing. These are social situations that are not
covered in the usual books.

Sometimes it's best to do nothing...

...like when you discover a pair of panties outside your neighbor's door.

My first reaction was to be helpful: pick them up, knock on the door, and hand them to my neighbor.

Fortunately, I have a censoring component in my brain that told me this would be the wrong thing to do. After all, if a stranger handed me my underwear, I'd be a little uncomfortable. It would be weird, and not just because I don't have any.

Okay, I thought, *what else then?* Knock on the door, leaving the panties where they lay? Not much better, really.

Knock and run? Nay, for that will mean she will feel embarrassed each time she sees *any* of the neighbors, since she will never know which one of us saw her panties.

I even thought about picking them up and running, just to save her the embarrassment of finding out she left her panties outside for all to see. But if I was successful, she'd be out a nice pair of purple panties. And besides, I figured she'd open the door just as I picked them up and I'd be branded a pervert.

No, there was simply nothing to do but leave them there.

A few minutes later, while I was in my apartment, I heard her boyfriend knock on her door. "Lose something out here?" he asked

"Oh! Those were—" (this is where the door slammed shut).

I could hear them laughing loudly, through the wall, probably quite confident that a nearly paralyzing faux pas had been avoided. And I went silently into the future, keeping it solemnly to myself that I know the color of my neighbor's panties.

Shh!

That was just a weird series of weeks. Panties
showing up everywhere. Not just any panties,
either. These were sexy panties of fine quality.

People should really keep better track
of their alluring underwear

Today it was a pair of thong panties—pink, some lace, but not slutty or anything. Immaculate, as usual. And very sexy. They are on the table, in the laundry room, in case that person is reading this.

Also, someone left a caramel filled chocolate bar on the red fire alarm box-thingy.

Yeah, you both know who you are. Go get your stuff.

With this short piece, I was exploring
the idea that because we get to know
people online without interacting
with them in real life, there is this
sort of imagined relationship between
everyone. There is a sort of made-up
connection that can be very intimate
or not very intimate at all, and you can
never know for sure how intimate the
other person thinks your relationship is.

      I suppose it's true in real life
relationships, also, though there is
usually less guess work involved.

You Are Not Wearing Any Clothes

In fact, neither am I.

Oh sure, you appear to be draped in some
sort of fabric. But deep down...you are naked.
What's more, you are fellating me wildly while I
give you oral pleasure.

I just wanted you to know. Deep down. That's
what's happening.

I have no idea what I was thinking when I wrote
this, but it sounded dirty. And it was entertaining.
And yet, it shouldn't sound dirty because a spork
is just a harmless plastic element. But that is not
how language works, I guess. Things can *sound*
dirty even though they are not and things can *be*
dirty and still sound rather clinical and boring.

I am so going to spork you

Whether it be while you are sleeping or during your daydreams, rest assured: it will happen.

There is nothing you can do. Each of you, as you read this, will feel the oncoming dread, the crystal-clear realization that you will be sporked. You may as well accept it.

Or, go to the library and cower in a quiet, dank, musty corner where they shelve the oversized books that no one knows about (except for the fact that I have just told you). Perhaps, I will be waiting for you there.

Some readers suggested that people leave cling
wrap because they know you'll be wrapping up
food since you just moved in. However, I have
trouble believing this because people are not
usually very thoughtful. And besides, what food
would I be wrapping up? I just moved in! Who
needs to wrap up pizza?!

Cling Wrap: What Is It Good For?

The last two places I've moved into both contained an auspicious roll of cling wrap, left behind by previous inhabitants. Also, there was ice in the ice trays and a small amount of toilet paper in each bathroom. The ice and toilet paper I understand, but what was the courtesy of leaving plastic wrap all about?

I called my sister in absolute mystery. She's a genius and lives in the desert, so I knew she would have the answer.

She explained all about the traditional move-in dance that has to be performed while wearing nothing but cling wrap.

Well, I apologize for my ignorance, for in all my thirty years I had never performed such a thing!

I followed her directions exactly and received the traditional gawks, stares, shrieks of alarm and disparaging remarks about my genitalia. I also received the honorary arrest, beating, cavity search and free night in jail that my sister said would only happen if I was an outstanding success.

I feel as though I have been initiated into another amazing facet of human life. Success!

I just want to set the record straight, in case
people get the wrong impression about me. I
like cats. I like animals. I'm not one of those
squealing humans that gets excited whenever they
see a dog, but I like animals. Cats, in particular,
have helped me out from time to time with their
spiritual wisdom. Spiders, too. Yes, I like spiders.
And I like plants. And LEGO bricks. But now I'm
off the subject....

Cats: What Are They Good For?

Here's one thing: stopping floods.

If you have enough of them (and they are dead), a pile of cats makes a good levee.

Don't try to use live ones because that means you have to put a bunch of them into burlap sacks and they will try to scratch you while you do it. This also takes extra time, and come on, the floodwaters are rising.

This really happened. I doubt it was Kate
Beckinsale, but sometimes...well...I can't help
but think there were some odd details that I have
trouble explaining, otherwise. Maybe it was some
other Kate. I don't know. In either case, she was
quite beautiful and she liked my trench coat. I
don't think I've ever had a girl compliment me on
that trench coat before, so thanks, whoever you
are.

As Scotty and I left the party, she was
smoking with one of her henchmen over on the
side of the building. I looked back as I walked,
and waved. She waved back.

A few blocks later, Scotty threw up.

The Night I May or May Not Have Met Kate Beckinsale, Version 1

I was at the Second Annual G.I. Joe Party, held in the warehouse district of Denver.

A sentry at the door inspected me to make sure I was dressed in military garb—I was dressed as an "assassin," which meant that I wore all black (which meant that I had no military garb to wear). I did, however, have a kickass, European, military-style trench coat (which, incidentally was not black, but gray, and was made of wool).

Pretty late in the party, a woman entered that looked exactly like Kate Beckinsale. She was the hottest woman there and was flanked by two protective males.

All three of them got in without military costumes and they stood apart from the crowd, not knowing anyone there.

I didn't really think that much of it and decided to join my friend, Scotty, who was outside with the smokers, getting fresh air.

Well, within a few minutes, guess who comes out to smoke: the Kate Beckinsale look-alike, of course. She asks me for a light. She asks Scotty for a light. Finally, she gets a light from the guy next to Scotty.

We politely go around and say our names, trying not to drool over the hot chick.

When it's her turn, she says, "I'm Kate."

I say, "You look like a Kate."

"I should think so," she answers.

See, that's a British way of saying that. She didn't have an accent that I could tell, but Americans don't go around saying, "I should think so."

Maybe she was stuck in Denver that night because her jet had to be repaired or something, and her two "handler" men took her out and tried to find something different and exciting to do—sometimes quite a challenge in Denver.

Though, perhaps it was some woman named Kate, who didn't know anyone at the party that night, who liked to use British phrases and intonations without pronouncing words in a British way and who happened to look exactly like Kate Beckinsale.

Oh yeah, so what happened after we introduced ourselves? We talked for a few minutes and that's about it. She did compliment me on my trench coat, though, which is really the point of this story: I have a kickass trench coat.

And Scotty puked on the way home.

The Night I May or May Not Have Met
Kate Beckinsale, Version 2

It was a hot night. I was drunk. Everyone at the party was on something. An orgy ensued in several of the bedrooms upstairs. It's possible that Kate Beckinsale took part in them.

Okay, so it's true that I was downstairs the whole time and didn't take part in any orgiastic fun. But it's also true that Kate Beckinsale, if she had been at that party, may have come downstairs for a break at some point.

And I met a lot of people that night that I can't remember, so you could say it's possible that I may have met Kate Beckinsale.

I liked the title so much I had to turn this into a trilogy.

I wanted to go over the top on the last one. I think there's a good joke or two here, such as the last line, punctuated by, "if it's a celebrity." I'm just demented enough to think that's funny. I know some of my readers are, too.

May 26, 2005

The Night I May or May Not Have Met
Kate Beckinsale, Version 3

Once, aliens abducted me and made me have sex with a woman.

She didn't look anything like Kate Beckinsale, but I've read that aliens can make you think that people look like other people, so it's possible that I could have been having sex with Kate Beckinsale and not even known it.

So I guess I didn't really possibly "meet" Kate Beckinsale so much as possibly insert my penis into her vagina, but I think that should count, if it's a celebrity.

I was bored when I watched *Close Encounters of the Third Kind* as a child. As an adult, all I could think about was what a cad the guy was. He has this encounter with aliens and suddenly he turns into a moron who doesn't care about his family.

And what's with the game of Simon Says? Aliens are going to travel all this way to play a silly game? Heh. I thought that was hilarious.

September 5, 2005

My Close Encounter With That One Movie

So, I recently watched that Steven Spielberg movie from way back for the first time since I was very small and I had a few gripes.

Though I do agree that there are a lot of dads who run off and willingly go into space, leaving their wife and children behind, I think it's fairly unlikely that aliens would travel to our planet just to play a game of See-If-You-Can-Remember-These-Five-Notes-And-Play-Them-Back.

Also, the film left a few things unexplained. For one: will there be a fourth kind? And what happened to the first and second? I just want to know.

I write a lot of stories that are straight out of my dreams. This one is not so entertaining except for the fact that I was able to get an entertaining title out of it, which ties the piece together and makes it worth reading. Sometimes a blog is worth writing, just for the title.

A Mosquito Destroys What Is Left Of My Sex Life

So I'm having a dream, right? I'm at this pretentious place having dinner with an off duty male cop and we each have foxy dates.

Now, this place is so pretentious that for some reason I had to have three bouquets of flowers to place on the table just to be served. They had no qualms about explaining just how this should be done, too.

We order and I have this fake pork chop for some reason (it was okay), but while we eat, the snooty waiter describes some sordid night just like this one (rainy or something, I don't know) where some cop was at their restaurant and a call came in on his radio about someone running a stop sign. Well, the cop didn't do anything about it and the guy that ran the stop sign ended up causing a horrible car accident.

I was like, "Jeez, guy, leave us alone, will ya'? We're eatin' here!" Except I didn't really say that because I'm not from Jersey.

This snooty waiter obviously didn't like us. He also told us we had to consume all the food on the premises (no doggie bags) because they had had problems with people taking the food home to conduct experiments on it.

Then, on a police scanner that happens to be sitting nearby, a nosy neighbor called in someone running the stop sign just outside the restaurant.

And the waiter guy was all, "Are you going to do something about that?" to the cop.

And the cop was all, like, "Uh...yeah."

And he stood up and got out his little radio thinger that allows him to talk to dispatch and then this mosquito buzzed by my ear and woke me up, which I was really upset about. I know it was only a dinner date, but I was really hoping to score 'cause it has been a while.

Thanks a lot, stupid mosquito!

You know you've been spending too much time
online when you start dreaming about people
you've never met in real life. I woke up and
thought, *what was Gary Robert Smith II doing
in my dream?* It's a little weird, but there he was,
conveniently looking just like one of his online
photos, obnoxious sunglasses and all. He is an
excellent writer and an excellent sport for letting
me post the blog and include it in the book.

   When I posted this I simply scanned the
pages out of the journal that I wrote it in. It's a
little difficult to read, so for this book I've also
included a typed version (turn the page).

It was a dream and I take NO responsibility

Gary R. Smith comes a little close to running over a dog at the side of a road. I wonder if he is on drugs. From the back seat I watch him ~~~~~ purposely veer for another dog and I think it's a goner but somehow he slows down swerves a little and slows down some more, inches past the dog and an irate dog owner. The dog owner is screaming at us but it doesn't matter.

We are in a convertible. I am only sort of half in, actually; there is not much of a back seat and we are in the country and speeding and drifting over the median.

We can do this and get away with it because we are cool. I must be Uma Thurman, or some other equally cool chick in the passenger seat next to Gary. My right leg snakes up between the bucket seats, resting next to her left arm while I sit on my other leg and wonder when we will all die: not today, though, I am sure, because we are cool.

Gary R. Smith comes a little close to running over a dog at the side of a road. I wonder if he is on drugs.

From the back seat, I watch him purposely veer for another dog and I think it's a goner but somehow he slows down swerves a little and slows down some more, inches past the dog and an irate dog owner.

The dog owner is screaming at us but it doesn't matter:

We are in a convertible. I am only sort of half in, actually; there is not much of a back seat and we are in the country and speeding and drifting over the median.

We can do this and get away with it because we are cool. It must be Uma Thurman, or some other equally cool chick in the passenger seat next to Gary. My right leg snakes up between the bucket seats, resting next to her left arm while I sit on my other leg and wonder when we will all die: not today, though, I am sure, because we are cool.

I can't help liking this piece. It just makes so
much sense. And it's so positive, too! The young
people aren't the death of law and order—they
have so much respect for the law that they are
double obeying it!

And That's Why My Dad Drives So Slow

You see, my father respects the law a good deal. I'd say he respects the law about 90 to 95%. That's why when he is driving a car in a 55 mph zone, you'll see him driving at 90 to 95% of that speed limit, thus he is generally always going around 5 mph slower than the limit.

Some days, his respect for the law drops to 80% and he can then be seen driving 10 under the limit. But eventually his appreciation for the law returns to its normal level.

And now, as an added bonus, I will explain to you how much I respect the law. I typically respect the law 120%. Thus, I must therefore drive at 120% of the speed limit. Obviously, this explains how much the younger generations have radically improved upon older generations' respect for the law.

The world is on an upswing, I tell you!

I wrote a lot of roadnotes during my first 18 months of blogging. I love to travel and I'm lucky enough to have friends everywhere, which makes the experience much more affordable.

I didn't include very many roadnotes in the book because they just didn't seem interesting enough to me. I know that some of my readers particularly enjoy them, but for the most part they are just self-serving ramblings. This series I thought was a little more poignant and crafted, so I included it.

Most of the roadnotes are written in my journal and then transferred to the computer when I get the chance. I've changed the dates on these to the days that I actually wrote them. They were usually posted a day or two after.

Roadnotes: Denver 1

Two days ago at my writer's workshop, there was surprise expressed, by several, that I, at age 31, had been to 15 or 20 funerals. I didn't think 15 or 20 was that many. Now I wonder how many is "normal."

The subject came up, of course, when I told them of my upcoming trip. The one I'm on now. I'm going to a funeral in Denver.

I'm not there, yet—I'm on a bus headed to SEATAC, wishing my suit and dress shoes didn't require me to take a full-sized carry on. Much easier to get around with just a backpack.

≡ :: ≡

I'm at the airport. A quick tour of food options has made me think that vegetarians don't travel much. I had to walk what seemed like half the length of the airport just to find something that wasn't a veggie burger.

Now, I'm watching a woman eat, one table over. She stares at the cover of a fashion magazine and finishes her food. Then she flips through the magazine, quickly and efficiently taking out all the postcard size ads that would inevitably fall out if she didn't do this.

I caught you, lady! See, we all do these little things but we usually don't consider that we are doing them for an audience. Enough, though. I'll leave her with her stack of postcard ads and quit writing. I'm not even there, yet....

≡ :: ≡

No, there's one last thing. (I'm wordy today.) Is anyone else a regular Frontier flyer? If you're over, say, 5'10", you have to stoop down to see underneath the overhead compartments in order to see the row numbers for your seat assignment.

My first time on a Frontier plane freaked me out—I couldn't see any row numbers, yet everyone else seemed to know exactly where to go. It was Twilight Zone-esque. I almost turned around and counted the rows behind me. I did figure it out, somehow, without asking, and for a while afterward it annoyed me whenever I flew Frontier. Now it makes me laugh. Just a little. Deep down inside, where no one can see.

≡ :: ≡

Okay. One last thing again. And this time I mean it. I'm too embarrassed to
bring a book out of my bag to read. I'm on the plane and I have a copy of *The
DaVinci Code*, but I feel like it'd be too cliché or just too stupid to show people
that I, too, have reduced myself to that level.

Of course, I haven't *really* stooped that low—I have to read it for a class I'm taking
next quarter. The class is called, "The DaVinci Code: A Contemporary Grail
Quest." Honest. I'm not keen on the book, but I am keen on the history that
the book is based on, which is what the class is about. Thus, I must read the
book—it's homework I've been given before the quarter has even started. Don't
ask me why, but I actually love this school.

Anyway, I have other, more dignifying, options: *The Elements of Style* and
Ouisconsin, a book of poems by one of my professors. I'm shutting up now. Who
knows—I may not have anything to say for the rest of the trip.

Roadnotes: Denver 2

My favorite story:

Four days before S_____ died, she decided she wanted a drumstick—one of those ice cream cones with the fudge coating and peanuts, etc. Her husband, Trapper, goes to get her one but he doesn't know what kind. So he just buys a box of every kind they have. It is beautiful logic.

It was actually starting to wear on me, all these
challenges. I was headed back to finish out
my last week of the quarter, involving a lot of
schoolwork. My friend had just died. I was
working on homework and I was eating and
noticed Kirby Puckett's face on the TV.

It probably would have ripped me up
more if it hadn't been so comical. I mean, when
things happen to you repeatedly and they're all
negative, you start thinking that someone's doing
it on purpose, just to mess with you. So I thought
it was kind of funny, at that point, for this entity to
take away my childhood baseball hero just to put
the final screw in my back. I was sad, but in my
delusional state, there was comedy there, in that
moment. Me, finishing a stiff drink, working hard
as usual, just about collapsed from emotional and
physical fatigue...and this mysterious foul entity
chose that exact moment to let me know that
Kirby Puckett was dead. It really couldn't have
fazed me less, after preceding events.

All the same, though, I'm glad my sister
called. Good timing, sis. Thanks.

Roadnotes: Denver 3

It's been one long day ever since S_____ died, but everything has gone as well as possible. I guess.

Thanks to Quinn and Penelope and Geekdork, I didn't have to worry about where to stay or about rides to and from the airport. And Trapper will make it. It will suck, but he'll make it.

There is beauty, you know, still. The service was amazing and Trapper kept saying that during it, he could feel so much love....

There is comedy, too. During an intense conversation with S_____'s family this afternoon, cell phones kept going off and they all had the most inappropriate ring tones. When one rang the tune of "The Entertainer," it was all I could do to keep from cracking up.

I'm at the airport now, starved. And I'm temporarily stymied when I get to Concourse A because Panda Express is closed for remodeling. I've been in a non-vegetarian house for days so I wanted some fried rice with egg in it. Now I don't know what to do.

So, I pee. Does anyone else think it's strange how those automatic flushing urinals always seem to know exactly when you're done? It's eerie. I shake off the last drops and before I can put it away, the flushing begins. It's like they have someone watching, that's how dead-on it is.

At some place called Jimmy's, my drink costs more than my dinner. I'm there because as much as I lamented the choices at SEATAC, there are even fewer options in DIA's Concourse A.

I can hear some floozy saying things like, "I'm legal. I mean I'm not *barely* legal or anything but I'm young." I want to tell her to just hump the married guy's leg—maybe then he'd get the hint faster.

The "pasta rustica" is actually so good it surprises me. The silverware surprises me, too—it's about as light as air and made of plastic, but it *looks* like silverware.

I'm finishing up some homework while I finish off my drink when I happen to look at the TV for a moment. I see Kirby Puckett's face and I get excited for news about my boyhood hero until I see the caption underneath: 1961-2006.

Fucking shit crap.

I pay the bill. I find my gate. I sit down and I get a phone call from my sister.

"Have you heard?" she asks.

"Yeah. I just found out. He was about the same age as S_____."

Growing up, my sister used to tease me by calling him "Kirby Spitbucket." Now, after all these years, she suddenly feels a little bad about that.

I tell her it's okay (and it is). If I believed in last straws, I'd have collapsed by now. And Kirby is no straw—he's much bigger than that.

I can take this, too. You may not know this, but you're helping me get through this. All of you. So I can take it.

I love you S_____. I love you Trapper.

I love you Kirby Spitbucket.

I love you, sis.

I'm back in Seattle, now. And I will sleep well tonight.

I'm as good as dead

Trust me, in a billion years or so I may not even be around anymore, so enjoy me while you can.

I used to follow sports quite a bit. Then I grew up
and got a life. Now I'm too busy and I suppose
I'm less interested, too. For some reason, I find
it dull to follow the lives of rich people. And in
professional male sports at that level, they are all
rich.

You have to admit: the sports headlines
would be pretty funny if they said things like,
MILLIONAIRE HITS HOME RUN IN NINTH TO
WIN GAME, or WEALTHY MAN MAKES PASS
TO WIN SUPER BOWL.

In case you're wondering, this really
happened. I tore up three Carney Lansford
baseball cards and he went 0 for 3. Sorry, Carney.
I really didn't think it would do anything.

June 15, 2005

I hand out batting titles as if by magic
(oh, and baseball sucks)

In 1989, the American League batting title came down to the last game of the season. "Who will win?" thought a few people who cared.

There were two stalwart men vying for the prize: Kirby Puckett, a rising star just coming into his prime, and Carney "Dinosaur" Lansford, an aging old hack from a time before baseball was invented.

I took it upon myself to give the title to Puckett, who obviously deserved it more (plus, Lansford already had one from, like, a century ago—back when he was good).

Wallah! Operation: Magic Title was an astounding success! On the final day of the season, Carney Lansford went hitless, while Kirby Puckett collected *two more* hits to take the batting title by a difference of almost .003!

And how did I accomplish such a thing? Well, I suppose it doesn't matter if the secret gets out, since baseball has since been turned into the world's most ridiculous auction (note to baseball owners: auctions are boring). See, Kirby Puckett played *real* baseball during a time when a slugging average of .500 meant something. Nowadays, they've got guys that can slug .700 in their sleep (their wives have testified to this).

Note: I am not criticizing ALL of baseball, just everyone that is in baseball that gets paid more than $300,000 a year. What? $316,000 is the minimum wage for a baseball player? Well, maybe I'm being harsh—I didn't take into account how expensive steroids can be.

Oh yeah, sorry—I was going to tell you a secret. How did I give Kirby Puckett the batting title?

Voodoo magic. I went through my entire baseball card collection and destroyed every single Carney Lansford baseball card I could find (which was only 3 because I really didn't have a very good baseball card collection).

As proof that my intervention altered reality in favor of Kirby Puckett, I will share with you a key detail about Carney Lansford's last game: he went hitless in 3 at-bats. Got it? I destroyed 3 cards, and he went 0 for 3. Bam!

Now, go forth and use this voodoo magic to destroy the game of baseball as we know it!

This was a terrific series to write, if for no other reason than I just love the title. The title was so good that I had to make it a trilogy.

Another great aspect of this trilogy is that the first two are true. That is indeed how earthquakes were artificially made. I like this one in particular because—come on, people, do we really need more sports stadiums? Why do people want to pay for them? Again? And again? I just don't see the point. But then again, I don't even follow sports anymore.

How To Start An Earthquake For Free

It's not really for free, but don't worry—you'll get taxpayers to pay for it.

First, suggest to your city that you need a new sports stadium. People are suckers for new sports stadiums, so that part should be easy. However, you should make sure they approve one that will have a gigantic dome. The dome is essential.

Next, wait around 24 or 25 years and then come up with a reason to tear the stadium down. Hey, here's a good reason: how about to make room for another sports stadium? Sounds good to me.

Tada! Apparently, the most efficient (cheap) way to tear down a domed stadium is simply to implode it, which means that the large dome will come crashing to the earth all at once.

If you're anywhere near a fault line, this should result in a seismic reaction to the tune of at least 2.0 on the Richter scale. For a larger earthquake, find a more stressed fault line or build a bigger, heavier dome.

If your plan goes as well as what happened in Seattle, taxpayers will be paying for your earthquake long after the new stadium is built!

I learned about this while I lived in
Denver. It seemed incredibly crazy
to me, but it's true.

How To Start An Earthquake For Free, Method 2

It's not really free—you'll have to own a chemical weapons manufacturing plant first. After you have that, though, all you need is the natural by-product of manufacturing chemical weapons: chemical waste.

Pump this chemical waste deep into the earth. How deep? Oh, I don't know—try to get it into the Precambrian layer. You don't really want to pay to dispose of this stuff anyway, do you? No, I didn't think so.

The slipperiness of this waste material will inspire some sliding of the plates down there which should produce some nice little earthquakes.

You can make matters easier for your local populace by pumping the chemical waste at a regular time each day, so they won't be surprised when the earthquakes hit.

If your plan goes as well as what happened in Denver, your local citizens will start saying, "Looks like it's time for the afternoon trembles!" as if it's water cooler talk.

Ah...the Incredible Hulk. Why is it that he was always being shot at by the military? I guess that's just what the military does in comics. They certainly couldn't pass trade sanctions against the Hulk, so I guess destruction was the only option left.

How To Start An Earthquake For Free, Method 3

It's not really free—you might need a gamma ray-emitting bomb or other such similar device. Check the garage.

First, detonate this device to become the Hulk. Be forewarned—this might kill you.

If you are still alive, proceed to the next step: get really, really mad. This will increase your mass somehow. I don't know how it works, exactly, but maybe it's explained in the comics somewhere. You'll get some help from the Army, because for some reason as soon as you get fairly large, helicopters, tanks and jet airplanes will try to kill you, which will only make you more angry.

Keep getting angrier and angrier until you are the size of...say...the moon.

Jump up and down.

I've always been impressed with Doctor Touching's ability to express true sentiment (and even wisdom) through the computer user language of his Melnet posts. Those posts speak volumes about how self expression does not have to be limited by technological language.

I had always wanted to try something similar, so when The Redhead suggested I write a blog about "how to hack into alternate universes," written in "4@xxor," no less, I couldn't resist making 4@xxor an imaginary interface.

Doctor Touching can be found at: touching.pointlessbanter.net

Hacking the Marvel Universe

The Redhead recently requested the following: "I would like a blog about how to hack into alternate universes. (You can write it in 4@xx0r if you like.)" So, in the style of Doctor Touching's Melnet posts, I have answered the call of the hero.

```
run C:\4@xx0r.exe
loading.........
4@xx0r: whackjob//
4@xx0r-->whackjob//^dud@34s: ******
4@xx0r-->d!d: 200605280318d^@s)dkd
4@xx0r-->whackjob//: !6dfd@er4(4@xx0r,engusa)
4@xx0r-->Rput: USA English loaded
4@xx0r-->whackjob//: load(comicHacks,'C:\support4xx0r\')
4@xx0r-->Rput: loading...
4@xx0r-->Rput: comicHacks loaded
4@xx0r-->whackjob//: selUverse(Marvel)
4@xx0r-->Rput: Err(13)|Missing parameter(1,universeNo)|
4@xx0r-->whackjob//: selUverse(Marvel,0)
4@xx0r-->Rput: Universe=Marvel.0
4@xx0r-->whackjob//: selCharacter(Magneto)
4@xx0r-->Rput: Character=Marvel.0.Magneto
4@xx0r-->whackjob//: displayGenitalia(Character)
4@xx0r-->Rput: Magneto
   version=0
   testicles=2
   penis=1
   vagina=0
4@xx0r-->whackjob//: hackGenitalia(Character,testicles++)
4@xx0r-->Rput: Marvel.0.Magneto updated
4@xx0r-->whackjob//: displayGenitalia(Character)
4@xx0r-->Rput: Magneto
   version=0
   testicles=3
   penis=1
   vagina=0
4@xx0r-->whackjob//: Ha ha! I've changed the Marvel universe!
4@xx0r-->Rput: Err(2)|Misspelled command()|
4@xx0r-->whackjob//: Yer stupid!!!
4@xx0r-->Rput: Err(2)|Misspelled command()|
```

```
4@xx0r-->whackjob//: deSelCharacter
4@xx0r-->Rput: Marvel.0.Magneto deselected
4@xx0r-->whackjob//: deSelUverse
4@xx0r-->Rput: Marvel.0 deselected
4@xx0r-->whackjob//: saveUverse(Marvel,0)
4@xx0r-->Rput: Marvel.0 updated
4@xx0r-->whackjob//: logout
4@xx0r-->d!d: 200605280327d^@s(dkd
End
```

December 22, 2005

You have to be smarter than smart
to be considered smart

...because the test is written by someone much less intelligent.

It's kind of like what Nicholson Baker said about John Updike. Updike is more than genius because he can make his genius understandable. You see, if you have a genius concept and you want to get it across to stupid people, you have to be even more genius than the original concept: *double* genius!

That's what you're up against, smart people.

One day, I was intrigued by a random thought:
what if Spiderman decided to market his web-
shooters commercially? Of course, most people
wouldn't have the dexterity or aim to use them
well, but that probably wouldn't stop them from
trying.

This blog tackles the subject assuming
that people *can* use them. So then you have
other problems because of the sheer number of
people in the city. Can you imagine? Instead of
traffic jams, you would have web jams. People
would get each other stuck in webbing all over the
city, hanging there. They would probably need
emergency relief until the webbing dissolved. I
expect the National Guard would have to be called
in.

JUNE 17, 2005

The Problem With America's Future Alternative Method of Transportation

Don't get me wrong—I'm a big fan of Peter Parker's invention: The Web Swinger Personal Transportation Device (WSPTD).

It is definitely the best way to get around the city right now. It's a big place and you can't beat the speed of web swinging—probably not even with a race car on empty streets. I was able to get from Greenwich Village to Harlem in less than two minutes! That's pretty incredible!

Now it does have some immediately noticeable drawbacks, like, you need to have quick reflexes to dodge all the traffic lights and wiring. However, after my second or third concussion (remember: always wear a helmet), I pretty much got the hang of it.

The following are the primary reasons why I did not buy stock during the IPO: Think about it: one or two people swinging around Manhattan is no problem, but there are *millions* in need of fast transportation! Oh, what a tangled web they will weave if they all use the WSPTD!

Plus, think about the rural populations. When Federal Express delivers Farmer Joe's WSPTD, won't he be disappointed when he learns it's really hard to web sling into town without any buildings around? And Farmer Joe is representative of a large share of the market: Ninety percent of America is rural, or so I read about 150 years ago and I'm sure that number hasn't changed *too* much.

On the positive, though, the ugly web residue left behind from using this device biodegrades in three years. Way to go, Peter Parker!

I've included my very first blog, not because it was
all that good, but because it's interesting to see
what I started doing and what I ended up doing.

The following piece came about when a
friend requested in an email, "Write me something
about small things." I wrote her back, and later
I thought it would make a decent blog. Thus, my
first blog was born.

Incidentally, as I'm writing this, my
shoelace is about to break again.

My shoelace will soon break...

Over the past few weeks, I've noticed a spot where the color has turned white and the lace is frayed on an otherwise smooth, black shoelace. Each morning as I tie my shoes, I think, "Is this the morning that my shoelace will snap?" But I pull it taut and nothing happens. I tie the bow and go to work.

But sooner or later it will break and I have done nothing to prepare for the event. I am normally a very good planner. I don't run out of Kleenex, toilet paper, milk, orange juice, parmesan, or any other daily supplement. But I have a problem planning for broken shoelaces because I never know what length of shoelace to buy.

I can go to the store, count my number of eyelets, and estimate using the helpful guide on the back of the packaging, but either because I buy boots or because I have skinny feet, this does not give me the right length of shoelace.

For a while, I would go to the store, estimate from the number of eyelets, then buy a range of shoelaces, three or four pair, just to make sure I had the right length.

But now I've discovered that I prefer to wait until they break. At that point, I unlace the broken shoelace, then lay the two pieces out to measure them. Then, when I go to buy the shoelace (walking strangely, so that my shoe does not fall off), I know that I need a 45 inch shoelace, or a 54.

Of course, there is the inconvenience of having an unlaced shoe until I make it to the store, but that is another story.

For some reason, I thought it
incredibly important to update
people on the shoelace situation.

My shoelace didn't break

I replaced my shoelaces today. But I swear one was getting very close to snapping.

This was based on an actual letter my friend
received placing him on "investigatory leave." I
was, at the time, not even sure if that was a word,
but I looked it up. Sadly, it *is* a word and even
more sadly, people use it.

      As for the title and the screwed up
English...well, it wouldn't be a funny title
otherwise. I love language that is messed up
and primal. It sounds more expressive that way,
sometimes.

If you want use the word investigatory, please to use the word investigative instead

I mean, duh. "Investigatory" is such an ugly word, and I can't think of a time when you couldn't use "investigative" instead.

"Investigatory" requires more syllables added on to make it acceptable for use, as in "investigatorial," which is a word for an investigative editorial. It is also acceptable to use the word, "investigatoratamus," since we all know that investigativatamuses don't exist.

So, please do not put employees on "investigatory leave." Instead, put them on "investigative leave." It sounds so much better.

Thank you.

It's okay with me if you want to use the quotation marks. Those are optional.

This piece is, of course, absurd, but it has a bit of
a point. This whole Internet speak, particularly,
drives me crazy. Is LOL really expressive of
anything?

And here is what I don't like about "new" words that are basically just abbreviations

Like, shepherd, for instance. I suppose at one time people used to say "sheep herder" and that got shortened to "sheep herd".

What bonehead decided that we could save ourselves writing out one more letter and call it "shepherd"? No one herds sheps!

Ooh, they saved the English-speaking human race, there, freeing us from having to deal with one more letter. I bet in the course of my lifetime, this may very well add up to 10 seconds.

Oh, and here is another of my favorites: blog

My goodness, that saves us all two keystrokes! Genius! And it sounds stupid, too!

I mean, if you're going to invent a new word that is just an abbreviation of a word or words that already exist, go the distance. Don't just save us 10 seconds over the course of our lives, save us 30 or 40!

Here's an idea: what about "sherd," as a new word for "sheep herder." That's *way* more efficient.

And here's my new word for "weblog": bl

That's right, "bl". That's all you need.

Imagine how much time you'll save in conversation not having to augment your mouth into that nasty "OG" sound. Ugly, isn't it?

Instead, you can just say to your friends, "Yeah, I finally got a bl up the other day about last weekend when I passed out."

In fact, if I were to have my way, the previous sentence above could really be abbreviated to: "Y, I fin gt bl up t'oth dy bt lst knd wn I psd ut."

See? You already know what I'm talking about!

And if these are the kinds of things you want your children to learn, make sure to elect me president during my first year of eligibility (2012). Vote for Arn!

I'm always looking at my writing and finding
ways to improve it. Limiting a language's choices
makes that process easier. For this blog I took
that concept to the extreme. I created a one-word
language and explored the potential of a "perfect"
piece of writing.

It's an interesting subject to *me*, anyway.

The Writing Twilight Zone:
The One Word Language

I consider all of my writing works-in-progress. It's not possible to write something that is perfect, something that cannot be improved upon in some way. However, there are varying degrees away from perfection that one can achieve. If you are very good (better than me), you can be very much relatively close to perfection, whatever that means.

However, what if we simplified the language somewhat? Would perfection be any easier?

Consider: a language with only one word. Perhaps it is written like this:

THE

Perhaps, given this limitation, we might express the most perfect work of art that can be expressed in that language like this:

THE

It is as perfect as the language allows. Could the work be improved by adapting it to other languages or using images? Probably. But given the limitations of that language, it has the highest percentage of perfection possible.

...though, this could be argued. The work is the most concise way to say the one word that the language makes available, but some would prefer a longer story. Brevity is not always the most masterful technique with which to get a point across (much to my frequent chagrin). Some would prefer the following:

THE THE THE

Or even:

THE THE THE THE THE THE THE

Which one is more perfect? Is it brevity or style that counts? Oh, the wily whims and subtleties of perfection!

This was sort of an unplanned sequel to the previous blog. I was busy doing some things around the apartment on a Saturday afternoon and this just popped into my head: I will write a blog in the one word language!

Some people got it. Others thought I had flipped. Both reactions are valid.

THE THE THE THE THE

THE THE THE

THE THE THE THE THE THE

THE THE THE

THE

THE

THE

THE THE THE THE THE THE THE THE THE THE THE THE THE THE THE THE THE
THE THE THE THE THE THE THE THE THE THE THE THE THE THE THE THE THE
THE THE THE THE THE THE THE THE THE THE THE THE THE THE THE THE THE
THE THE THE THE THE THE THE THE THE THE THE THE THE THE THE

This could have fallen flat but people really really
seemed to get it. I mean, some didn't. But some
did. They beeped back and I beeped back again
and suddenly we were all beeping. People really
can communicate in beeps, you know.

I Am Robot, Hear My Beep!

BEEP

A reader who went by the name of Tourné commented on this one, saying, "But what about Keats? He died in his twenties."

I responded, saying, "Keats may kick my ass, but at least I'm not dead!"

I am a shitty writer

Whenever I think about how shitty my writing is I want to puke.

Then I try to think about all the great writers who didn't write anything good until they were 40.

And then I think, "Heheh. I may suck at writing, but at least I'm not 40 years old!"

I had to save this one for the end because I wanted you to get through the entire book. Now, after reading this, you will realize that you have better things to do. I guess I can let you go now. Good luck.

MARCH 6, 2005

By my own genius,
I will save you from a pointless existence

So, I was reading a book yesterday (*The Rover*, by Joseph Conrad) and it inspired me to write, so I set down the book to write, but first I thought, "Why wasn't I writing in the first place?"

I had the ability to write (fairly cognitive processes, pen, paper, arm, hand, fingers, etcetera). I just didn't think about how I wanted to write until I read the book.

So I realized, why didn't I just inspire myself to write without having to read the book? It's as simple as that!

It's like that time I saw *American Beauty* and it inspired me to go back to school and hit on chicks even though I was way older than them. I could have decided to go back to school and hit on chicks without even seeing the movie! I'd have saved myself two hours, and probably around 10 bucks, too!

So, this is my point: all you have to do is decide what you want to be inspired to do at any given moment, and then go do it. You don't have to read. You don't have to see movies. Just go do what you've been wanting to do.

I don't want to see any of you reading this book ever again. I have just defeated its purpose for you. I expect you all to be living highly actualized lives within minutes.

Now go. And never come back.

THE THE

The Author

Aaron Dietz lives in a haze of random infatuation and misguided, self-invented jurisprudence. On a cloudy day, you might imagine his face in the sky, especially if you don't know what he looks like, because then just about any cloud will do. He has a friend that always wants him to play "House of the Rising Sun" on guitar every time Aaron visits, but thus far, Aaron has never learned the song.

The writings of Aaron Dietz can be found at:
aarondietz.us
aaaaaaron.pointlessbanter.net

The Artist

Erik Tosten is an artist out of Dallas, Texas who bides his time between teaching and pining for success in the art market. While not a native of Texas, he is starting to take a liking to his new environment. He is originally from the greener pastures of Iowa, specifically Ames.

To find out more about this strange creature, check out the Web site dedicated to his life's work:
etosten.com

Printed in the United States
135604LV00002B/1/A

9 781847 288011